ISBN 978-1535538923

Printed in the United States of America
First edition, 2016

For Our Story.

ÑØ MØRÈ MÅGÍ© WÅÑÐ$

Table of Contents

ÍÑTRØÐŪ©TÍØÑ 5

THÈ £ÅST WÍSH ØF HØÑÈST ÈYÈRGRÈÈÑ 10

ÍÑ THÈ SHÅÐØW ØF THÈ FÅTHÈR 18

MÍSTÈR GRØŪÑÐHØG 23

FÈÅR ØF Å PŪRRÍÑG ©ÅT 34

THÈ ÐÅÑ©ÍÑG SÅ£ÈSMÅÑ 41

THÈ FÍSHÈRMÅÑ ØF ßÍRÐS 53

THÈ ØRÍGÅMÍ MÅÑ 58

THÈ ÍÑTÈRYÍÈWÈÐ PÍG 68

THÈ ß£ÍÑÐ GÈÑÈRÅ£ ÍÑ THÈ FØRÈST 76

THÈ MÅÑ WHØ ÐÍÐ ÑÈXT TØ ÑØTHÍÑG 90

ßÅ©K TØ THÈ SPÍÐÈR'S ÑÈST 97

THÈ RŪÐÈ TÈÅ©HÈR 102

THÈ TRÈÈ ØW£ 108

THÈ WØMÅÑ WHØ FØŪÑÐ HÈRSÈ£F 117

ÅßØŪT THÈ ÅŪTHØR 128

ÍÑҬ®ØĐŪ©Ҭ́Í́ØÑ

Security is everyone's job.

That's what we say as security professionals, but we don't always act like we believe it. It really does take everyone working in concert to make an organization truly secure. Why, then, do we do so little to enable those outside the cybersecurity field to do their part of the universal security job? We often provide some training, usually in the form of mandatory twenty-minute propaganda videos. But what about tools? Maybe we create a button to encrypt email data or to report phishing. What about books? Mostly we just provide a bunch of technical reference manuals, white papers, or standards written for the highly technical security professional. In them are policies that no one ever reads.

If security is everyone's job, everyone needs to have the right tools to actually do the job. Not *some* of the tools. Not *a little bit* of the information. All of it.

In cybersecurity, all of us are on the frontlines of a complicated battle involving governments, organized crime, activists, and more, which makes the notion that security is everyone's job even more important. If that's your goal, you must empower your employees to take initiative. They should be able to think for themselves. They should not have to constantly ask for direction. If you always tell people exactly what to do and how to do it, they'll never develop the ability to be self-directed. This is why cybersecurity should entail real-world, experienced-based training—not just awareness—to create a culture of ownership. Annual training should be progressive, and its lessons should build on each other over several years. The company should provide real examples of cybersecurity issues in order to give the training efforts a specific direction and focus. If the training involves reading from a binder or sticking to a narrow script, what will happen when something off-script happens? Employees won't know how to react and will have to ask for input from their supervisors.

If we improve our communal awareness of cybersecurity, we can start to develop a kind of collective immunity to cybercrime. Today, it is cheap and easy to be a cybercriminal: software isn't difficult to hack, and people make easy targets. This means that victims are plentiful, and the risks of getting caught or prosecuted are extremely low. However, if the cost of cybercrime increases and the chances of getting caught go up, the volume of cybercrime will be forced down (assuming cybercriminals' ill-gotten profits remain the same).

There needs to be an ecosystem of participation in security so that salespeople, accountants, attorneys, bankers, doctors, librarians, barbers, and car salesmen can all communicate with one another about the types of cybercrime they've experienced: How they were hacked and what they did to improve their security measures. Which technologies worked and which ones didn't. Which common techniques hackers are employing today. Everyone should be able to look to the security community for leadership and find answers.

Great cybersecurity is possible, but it's not easy.

Have you ever felt like someone was asking you to wave your magic wand at a problem and make it go away? You may have wanted to shout, "It's not that easy!" This is what's happening in cybersecurity. Wave your magic wand and everything will be better? Not in real life. If there really was a magic wand to be found, then thousands of companies wouldn't become the victims of cybercriminals every year. Software could be made to run perfectly, business processes would be designed without loopholes, everyone would follow policy, and employees would be constantly vigilant. Cybercrime would be a thing of the past.

This book imagines what life would be like for a magic-wand manufacturing company, staffed entirely by elves, after knockoff wands with their label start cropping up. On top of that, their customers' private information gets leaked and becomes scattered all across the enchanted forest. But the elves still have one magic wand. Can they use it to fix the mess? Or will they have to think of something else—some other way to prevent the villains of the enchanted forest from going one step further and stealing their greatest treasure?

The unlikely hero isn't a security guy. She's a business elf who makes it her mission to change the way her company does business from the top down. One of the first things she does is build a coalition of partners inside and outside the business to help make those changes happen. She looks for other fairy-tale creatures who have had personal or professional experiences with cybercrime and who have taken to heart the hard lessons of being hacked. She considers weathering the trials of being hacked a badge of honor, not a failure on their part. She has to learn how to talk to other business creatures about security—and she has to do it in their language, not her own. On her quest, she must challenge people to change their ways before the next breach happens. She does this by simulating a hack on the company, thereby creating the learning experience of being breached without the negative consequences. In this new world, she learns that it needs to be okay for people to challenge authority, even when it might normally be considered rude. Without a culture of inquiry and vigilance, actual security will be out of reach. She realizes that, just like a healthy immune system, there need to be multiple interconnected structures inside the organization to keep things working together.

This book isn't just written for technology professionals, although it may help them. It's written for anyone and everyone who wants to make a difference and improve cybersecurity. The first lesson that students of cybersecurity learn is that there's a constantly evolving cycle of improvement. Although basic principles will remain the same, you must always grow and adapt to various threats as they emerge. You will never arrive at a state of perfect security.

No matter how good you are, you will be hacked at some point.

It may be a surprise to hear, but hackers are an important part of the security environment. Hackers help the security ecosystem improve, particularly when they reveal the vulnerabilities they find or disclose the methods they used to expose weaknesses in a company's security measures. Imagine a young infant: we don't *want* the baby to get sick but, if she were never exposed to germs, her immune system wouldn't properly develop and she could wind up being very weak and vulnerable later on in life. Without hackers, our cyber immune system wouldn't develop and could be susceptible to worse cyber threats: attacks from government-sponsored actors, large-scale organized crime, or malicious inside jobs.

Finally, and perhaps most importantly, cybersecurity successes should be celebrated. This could mean giving incentives to employees for meeting their security objectives for the year or it could mean paying bounties for finding vulnerabilities. It could mean having an annual awards banquet where you recognize and reward individuals who contributed to improving cybersecurity in meaningful ways. However you celebrate, it should be something memorable. Make it something people will talk about all year long.

Changing the culture of an organization isn't something that any one person can do alone, but it is something that can be accomplished together. This book is a starting point for you and your team to begin building your plan.

THE LAST WISH OF HONEST EVERGREEN

Once upon a time, there lived a wood elf known as Honest Evergreen. He was an average elf in every way: he lived in a tree like the other wood elves, he enjoyed eating berries, and he worked on storing pecans in his basement for the winter. But Honest Evergreen had a gift that no other elf had.

One spring morning, Honest Evergreen was absentmindedly whittling a stick to pass the time. The flowers were blooming, the birds were singing and, before Honest knew it, the sun was beginning to ease its way back behind the hillside.

Honest looked down at the stick in his hand and was surprised to see that he had carved a wand. The handle was round and bumpy. Farther up, the wand curved and swirled, ending in a rather lovely star.

He chuckled and tossed it into the leaves as he turned to make his short walk home. Just then, he saw something out of the corner of his eye. The wand was sparkling. Bewildered, Honest moved to get a closer look. As he approached the wand, a nearby frog up leapt on its hind legs and began singing! The song was "It's Not Unusual," made popular by Tom Jones. *"It happens every day. No matter what you say. You'll find it happens all the time."* The frog bellowed the lyrics in the deepest voice his little mouth could manage.

Honest picked up the wand. He flicked his wrist at a nearby cricket, who instantly began beatboxing to the same tune as the frog. *"Love will never do what you want it to,"* the frog continued, now more confident with his chirping accompanier. *"Why can't this crazy love be mine?"* The frog shot its tongue out, swallowed the cricket whole, and burped.

Honest was struck with a sudden realization: his wand was magic.

The next day, Honest met with a fairy who lived in the next tree over. She was excited by Honest's story and asked if he would consider making more wands to sell. He agreed, so she placed an order for three magic wands and promised to tell all of her friends. She did, and they were so excited that they placed their orders by the dozen. Honest couldn't make magic wands fast enough, so he brought in his daughter, Harmony, to help run the business.

"We need a division of labor," Harmony explained.

"What's that?" Honest asked.

"Instead of hiring a bunch of elves to carve wands one at a time, we should give each elf a different part of the process so it goes faster," Harmony said confidently. "The humans do it with cars. One elf will do the rough cut, the next will do the pull cuts, the one after that will pare the shaft, and then the last one will carve the handle."

"So we'll be able to meet all the fairies' orders by the solstice?" Honest asked.

"Easily," Harmony said. And they did fill all of the orders. More and more orders came in the years that followed, until the cave underneath Honest's tree was full of brass nickels and pecans and cashews and walnuts, all the currencies of the enchanted forest.

One day, one of the fairies stopped by the tree to return a defective wand. The Honest Wand Company had never had a defective wand, so Honest didn't know what to do. Confused elves sent the fairy from office to office until she reached the heart of the tree and found Honest himself. "Let me see the wand," he said, and the fairy handed it over. She folded her arms while hovering in mid-air in Honest's small office. He looked it over from top to bottom, tapped it on the side of his desk, and flicked it toward a lightning bug that had settled in the corner of the ceiling. "This isn't one of ours," Honest concluded. "It doesn't have our secret carving in the bottom, and the wood is a simple balsa. Not the stuff we use."

"I want my money back," the fairy shrieked. Honest handed her a thick copper shilling that took up most of one of his desk drawers. The fairy snatched it and dragged it out the window.

Honest sent Harmony to investigate the market where the fairy said she had purchased the imitation wand. It was on the outskirts of the woods where the trees had been badly burned by a forest fire. Harmony discovered that the imitation wands were selling for half the price of Honest's wands, and they were sealed inside fancy packaging so the customer couldn't test the wand before purchasing it. Worse still, the market had hundreds of sales gnomes who would run away after a sale, always yelling, "No refunds!"

"Of course, it's possible that someone else independently happened upon the secret to making magic wands," Honest said to

Harmony. "The carvings are very similar, but the wood is cheap. You'd have to completely redesign it to make it work with that kind of wood. And, even then, it wouldn't last." Honest hung his head and closed his eyes, deep in thought.

"The fairies just think these are used and out of juice. The knockoffs are hurting our brand."

Just then, the very first fairy to whom Honest had ever sold a wand flew in through his office window, not waiting for an invitation. She was out of breath, and Honest walked over to her, concerned. The fairy held out her arm, flashing a look of sadness mixed with frustration, and opened her palm. In her hand were several pieces of rolled-up paper. They smelled like pigeon. The tiny scrolls were dotted with calligraphy, each listing two or three customer names and the types of wands they had purchased. Honest recognized the names of several notable elves from around the forest. "How did they get my customer lists?" Honest moaned.

Just then, an angry witch landed on the lawn in front of the tree. "Honest Evergreen!" Her voice boomed throughout the tree, shaking the leaves. "Honest Evergreen, come out here and face me." She cackled more threats, but they were drowned out by nearby thunder. The sky had begun to turn ominously dark just after the witch had landed.

Honest picked up his original magic wand from its perch on the wall behind his desk and walked down the stairs to the front door. The fairy and Harmony followed tentatively behind. As Honest approached the witch, he saw that she towered over him.

"Good day to you, madam." Honest's voice was welcoming. "I did not know witches knew about my magic wands. Your presence is an honor to us."

"The term 'witch' is derogatory," the witch sneered. "We prefer to be called magically inclined."

"No offense intended, madam. I've never met an, um, magically inclined person before."

"And you will never meet one again," the witch chastised him. "We in the Dark Coven have long preserved our secrecy. Until I bought a magic wand from you, I was nameless, faceless."

"Why would you need a magic wand?" Honest asked. "Since you are already magically incli—"

"Silence, elf. We in the Dark Coven seek all magic and its sources. My personal information has been exposed to the light of day, and my spells have led me to your doorstep. What say you?"

"This is my tree," the elf said in a commanding voice. "Its branches and roots all belong to me, and all the creatures inside act on my behalf. I promise you, on the life of my daughter, Harmony, this wrong will be made right."

"Those will be your last words, Honest Evergreen."

With her hands outstretched, she began to speak in a low, unnatural voice. "If two witches were watching two watches, which witch would watch which watch?" As she finished speaking, she thrust her palms toward Honest. A translucent wave of light moved toward the small elf. He flicked his wand at the light, and it shot upward, hitting a group of ducks that were flying overhead. Several ducks were instantly turned into giant yellow inflatable bath toys and tumbled to the ground.

Honest hung his head. Harmony and the fairy took a step toward him, but he motioned for them to stay back. All of his workers looked on in horror, and several of the forest's resident elves began to gather, waiting in anticipation for the battle of a lifetime. It would be a story that they could tell their grandbabies.

As it turned out, they *would* go on to tell the story of Honest, but it would be quite a different tale than what they expected at that moment.

The witch began mumbling another tongue twister. With her palms already facing outward, she began again, her voice now echoing on the wind. "Three sweet switched Swiss witches watch three washed Swiss witch Swatch watch switches. Which sweet switched Swiss witch watches which washed Swiss witch Swatch watch switch?" Lightning crackled from her fingers as she spoke and, as she uttered the last word, the electricity jumped toward Honest. As the sparks began to rain down around him, Honest raised his own wand and whispered something that no one else could hear. But instead of flicking his wrist, he held it steady, just to the side of where the lightning bolt passed into his chest.

At that moment, Honest began to grow and grow until he became the size of the witch, who watched in fearful horror. Just then, a gray haze passed over him, and he instantly turned to stone. The only thing that hadn't increased in size was the small magic wand, which was perched perfectly between the thumb and forefinger of the statue's grey stone hand.

The witch began to cackle and howl at the statue before her, but her laughter was cut short when she saw all of the elves and fairies form a circle around her and point their own wands at her. They waved their wands in unison, but nothing happened.

The witch hooted, hopping on one foot and then the other and dancing in a circle around the giant stone elf. "There are no more magic wands, you fools," she crowed. With that, she leapt on her broomstick and darted away, never to be seen again.

Summary

Honest Evergreen is like a lot of other CEOs after a company-wide security breach. They want to do what is best for the company, even if it means not being a part of it anymore. This is a noble thing. The company and its employees are the victims, but they're usually treated as if they brought the cyberattack upon themselves through their own ignorance. Ignorance requires a scapegoat or a sacrificial lamb. Usually, sacrificing a leader in this way means losing the leader's institutional knowledge. It also means disrupting leadership during a difficult time. All this makes a company more vulnerable.

There is hope, however. Honest made his sacrifice to protect his company but, as we'll see, he wasn't alone, and neither are you.

Takeaways

- Many great companies start with a magical idea and turn it into a reality. Sometimes, however, little thought goes into protecting that idea from competitors who want to steal the idea or hackers who want to expose or embarrass the company.

- In the aftermath of a breach, it can be impossible to know exactly what happened. It may take weeks of costly effort to discover the magnitude of the breach. But without this knowledge, it will be impossible to prevent it from happening again.

Questions

1. Was Honest right in sacrificing himself? What other options did he have?

2. In this story, who might the witch represent?

3. What data might you have in your company that thieves, competitors, activists, or governments might be interested in? How are you protecting that information?

ÍÑ ṪHÈ ṢḢÅÐØ₩ ØF ṪHÈ FÅṪHÈ®

Harmony Evergreen stood at the bottom of the statue, her head hanging low. The fairy floated by her side, holding a translucent umbrella over them both. The sun was setting, and an unnatural-looking cloud had formed around the statue, creating a mist over the clearing, as though the forest itself was shedding tears for the great elf. Honest Evergreen had never thought of himself as great, and his daughter knew it. If you had asked him, Honest would have said that he was just an average elf.

"Is there something we could have done differently?" Harmony asked the fairy, who responded by placing her free hand on Harmony's shoulder.

"It's not your fault," she said gently.

Harmony thought about the elves in the tree. She thought about all the fairies who had come to rely on the Honest Wand Company for their magic wands. She thought about the witch and what she would have done if she were in the witch's giant patent leather shoes. The leaks and forgeries hadn't just ruined Honest's reputation. They had made life worse for many, many forest creatures. What would the world be like without magic? "There has to be something we can do," Harmony said.

The last of the sun's rays began to grow brighter, dancing through the misty forest.

"Turn around, Harmony," the fairy said gently. Her wings buzzed as she pivoted to stand in front of Harmony.

Harmony turned around slowly, not wanting to betray the tears forming in her eyes. As she looked up, she saw a small rainbow. It began at the edge of the forest and ended in the palm of Honest Evergreen's outstretched hand—the one that held the magic wand.

Harmony spun and raced toward the base of the statue, grabbing handholds where she could. It was a long climb, and she slipped many times, but eventually she made it to where the rainbow ended. The wand was gently perched between Honest's fingers, and it shimmered in the waning light. It felt warm in Harmony's hands as she picked it up. It reminded her of how her father had first picked up the wand from where he'd tossed it in the leaves— a story that Honest had told her dozens of times over the years.

Harmony flicked the wand upward, and the clouds vanished. "It isn't true. The witch was wrong. There's still one magic wand left, and it's right here," she said to the fairy, who had flown up to meet her.

The fairy nodded slowly.

"I know what I need to do," Harmony continued, "but I need some answers before I do it. Let's find the wizard."

The fairy took Harmony's hand and stepped off the statue. Slowly they floated to the ground below, the fairy's wings buzzing heavily to guide them down safely.

"Where do we find him?" the fairy asked as their feet touched the ground.

"You don't find him," a strange and unfamiliar voice boomed from the canopy of a nearby tree. "He finds you." As he spoke, the tall wizard leapt from a limb of a nearby pecan tree. He glided toward Harmony on a gust of wind, and he landed in an easy stroll as though he had just begun his morning walk. "I know what you are planning to do, Harmony. And I don't like it."

"But will it work, Wizard?" Harmony asked.

"I cannot see the future, young Harmony Evergreen. Few have attempted the task you have set your mind upon. It is a great puzzle. Even if your wand can grant your wish, you must still solve a great mystery."

"What are you planning, Harmony?" the fairy asked nervously. "Your father wanted to protect us."

"And I want to return the favor," Harmony replied. "What if we could change what happened? What if people hadn't started copying our magic wands? What if someone hadn't stolen our customer information? Wouldn't things go back to the way they were before?"

"Maybe," the fairy said, "but you don't even know who stole all your information."

"You must first understand how it was stolen," the wizard explained. "*How* will lead to *who*, but I suspect that *who* doesn't matter so much."

"I don't understand," the fairy said, a little annoyed. "You've got a magic wand. Why can't we just wish the witch away?"

"You can't just wave a magic wand and solve all your problems. Dad taught me that much," Harmony answered. She looked up at the giant statue. Honest Evergreen's last action had been to not use magic at all. But why?

"Even if you manage to change the past—to stop the witch from casting the spell or prevent the thieves from stealing your design—someone else might come along later and steal it," the wizard said. "We might wind up at the same spot, standing beneath this statue." He placed a long pipe into his mouth and sent several puffs of smoke into the air. "You need to speak with the Groundhog, I think."

"I know the Groundhog," Harmony said. "He's one of our best managers, but he doesn't know anything about changing the past."

"Nobody knows about that. But he knows about running the company," the wizard answered with a wink, "and that is where you must start." He let out a large puff of smoke that billowed from his lips. Instead of dissipating into the wind as smoke usually does, it began to thicken, eventually surrounding the wizard. Then there was a loud popping sound, and the cloud of smoke vanished. The wizard was nowhere to be found.

Harmony took a deep breath and waved the wand over her head, sending herself backwards in time to before the customer lists were stolen.

Summary

Often, companies aren't prepared for a breach, and there's a real danger that the company could cease to exist after one occurs.

After a breach, a company has the opportunity to improve security by examining how the breach occurred. But what if you could predict threats and improve security before a breach happens? This is a much more challenging task, and it's what the remainder of this book will focus on. How do you change your security mindset from reactionary to proactive?

Takeaways

- There's no such thing as time travel. Most people wait until after a security breach to make significant changes. Opportunities for improving cybersecurity don't only come after a security breach. You'll need to be able to identify threats before they occur.
- There was a small spark of magic when your company was founded. You need to find that same spark and use it to ignite a fire that will change your company's cybersecurity mindset.

Questions

1. How can you become proactive about cybersecurity before a breach occurs?
2. Why can't the problems of the Honest Wand Company be fixed by magic?

MÍST̀È® G®ØŪÑÐHØG

The digital clock displayed a flashing 4:45 and was blaring a children's choir version of "Here Comes Santa Claus" when Mr. Groundhog thumped his wrinkled hand against it and sat up. He walked down the hallway to a room that he called his office, which was really just a small space with a treadmill in front of four wall-mounted TVs. He began jogging while watching the morning news—on four different channels.

Every day, he ran at his top speed for exactly twenty-eight minutes, giving him twelve minutes to shower and shave before making the thirty-minute ride to work. After his run, Mr. Groundhog fumbled with the white buttons on his dark navy pinstripe suit. He had just sewn the bottom button back into place the night before, and it was held tighter to the fabric than it had been in years. This made Mr. Groundhog stand up a little straighter as he left the house and ducked into the sleigh that was waiting for him. He bought a newspaper on the way to work, which cost him an extra five minutes. He arrived at the office exactly at 6 a.m. He wasn't surprised to see that his whole team was already there.

He was, however, surprised to see the person sitting at his desk. It was Harmony Evergreen. He paused briefly to check his red tie in the mirror; it was neatly in place. It wasn't every day that the daughter of the CEO paid a branch manager a visit.

"Mr. Groundhog, pleased to see you again," Harmony said with a quizzical smile.

"How can I help, Ms. Evergreen?" Mr. Groundhog asked.

"We have a problem," Harmony said.

Mr. Groundhog raised an eyebrow. He did not like problems. In fact, he had made it his life's work to not just eliminate problems but turn them into gold as well—quite literally.

Harmony explained that Mr. Groundhog would need to change the processes for his entire department because there was some kind of spy or information leak. Harmony referenced some vague story about trouble on the horizon and said the company could even go out of business one day.

Mr. Groundhog couldn't believe what he was hearing. His was perhaps the most profitable department in the entire tree. He had inherited dysfunctional branch after dysfunctional branch, whipping each one into shape and working his way up the tree. He had made it to where he was today by instituting the same business practices everywhere. Efficient, practical, scalable. Not only could he not accept that there was a mole in his department, he also couldn't believe the daughter of the CEO could be so paranoid about it.

He called in his secretary and asked her to cancel all his meetings for the day.

He spent the next ten hours with Harmony, discussing her concerns. Though his office door was closed, the workers outside could hear them arguing.

By the time Mr. Groundhog and Harmony finished, night had fallen, the secretary had gone home, and the office lights had long since been turned out. Mr. Groundhog looked out his window and let out a sigh. He scribbled something on a piece of paper and handed it to Harmony. The note read, "I quit."

The digital clock displayed a flashing 4:45 and began playing "Here Comes Santa Claus." Mr. Groundhog switched the alarm off and got out of bed. He ran, showered, and went to the office, stopping to get a newspaper on the way. The office was already buzzing with activity. This didn't surprise him. What did surprise him was seeing a person sitting at his desk. It was Harmony Evergreen. He paused briefly to check his red tie in the mirror; it was neatly in place and didn't need adjusting.

"Mr. Groundhog, pleased to see you again," Harmony said, a quizzical smile on her face.

"How can I help, Ms. Evergreen?" Mr. Groundhog asked.

"I've got a problem," Harmony began. "We're asking department heads from all around the company to review their practices. Change the business." Harmony leaned back into Mr. Groundhog's leather chair, which stretched and squeaked with the added pressure.

"You want us to change the business? I know this is your family's company, so I don't want you to take this the wrong way, but it's my company, too," Mr. Groundhog said as he stood up and looked out his window.

"I'm glad you feel that way, Mr. Groundhog," Harmony said confidently.

"We make the best magic wands," Mr. Groundhog said firmly. "The only magic wands. And we don't take advantage of our position. Our prices are reasonable, in part because we're efficient. Changing our processes will lead to inefficiencies creeping in. It will lead to increased prices. My team knows how good they are and are proud of the work they do. Changing will mean losing the culture that we've built. We could lose our position in the market, all because of a theoretical problem that might come up years from now."

"I understand. And this is why I need your help. I don't want to dictate how you should protect the company. I just wanted to make you aware of the problem so that you can put your understanding of the business to work."

"I appreciate your thinking of me, Harmony, but it sounds like you're just dumping a problem into my lap. I've got several meetings today, and I just don't have time right now to tinker with our processes. Why don't you come back with some more specifics so that maybe we can find a way to measure whether our changes will have any effect on the outcome?"

Harmony sighed.

"Mr. Groundhog, pleased to see you again," Harmony said, a quizzical smile on her face.

"How can I help, Ms. Evergreen?" Mr. Groundhog asked.

"I'm hoping I can help you," Harmony said, standing up give Mr. Groundhog a firm handshake. She placed her hand on his shoulder and led the way as they strolled about the office together. The workers' buzzing made the office sound like a beehive; it was loud, but Harmony and Mr. Groundhog kept talking. "You've got a track record of success, and I want to make sure we stay on track," Harmony said confidently. "We're looking ahead, and there are some signs of problems to come that we need to be prepared for."

Harmony explained the issues they were facing, giving several specific instances of customer lists being stolen from other companies and counterfeit wands starting to pop up in various marketplaces. "We need your expertise to help make sure this doesn't happen to us, but we also can't make drastic changes that will put us out of business."

"Are you thinking of expanding the business to crystal balls?" Mr. Groundhog asked. "That sounds like an awfully specific version of the future."

"It's actually more like a Magic-8 Ball," Harmony joked, "and it says the future is uncertain." Mr. Groundhog smiled at that. "What we really are looking for is to start a conversation. We will continue to bring you the intel we're getting from the field. We'll need to come up with some metrics on how to measure whether information is leaking out." Harmony watched as a giant caterpillar placed a twig into a large spider web in the center of the room. Seeing the twig, the spider jumped from her perch and began to spin it in her legs, trimming off all of its rough edges. When she was done, she slid the twig to the next workstation, where it passed in front of a children's wind-up robot with a very real hatchet in its hands.

"I have to admit that I've been thinking of making some changes to experiment with several processes," Mr. Groundhog said, walking down a row of desks where several elves were copying spells from one piece of paper to another. The finished spells were then carried by other elves to the end of the assembly line, where they were wrapped around the newly trimmed wand shafts to imbue the wands with longer-lasting magic. "I think we can start to incorporate some better protections into those processes so that we can measure the results before going full scale with our new methods."

"That makes sense," Harmony said. "Over time, we can begin to work on phasing in changes to stay ahead of criminals, but let's also take a prioritized approach." As she turned to walk back to Mr. Groundhog's office, a small elf stopped in front of Mr. Groundhog and deftly held out a clipboard with paperwork for him to sign.

"I think we'll probably need an extra resource here to help collect metrics and report on the results," Mr. Groundhog observed after a long pause.

"I can get that approved for you," Harmony said.

"And, to make sure we are still meeting our service levels, I'll need to be able to communicate with the other departments with whom we share information," Mr. Groundhog continued. "We'll need regular meetings and increased transparency on all of our numbers."

"Yes, that's a good idea," Harmony said, nodding. She noticed a smirk spreading across Mr. Groundhog's lips. "What?" she asked.

"I see what you're doing," Mr. Groundhog said, pointing his finger at her.

"What do you mean?" Harmony asked, frowning with the thought of replaying this whole day again. She reached into her purse and gently held the end of the magic wand, ready to use it again if she had to.

"You are buttering me up to get my help. Ho-ho-ho. By gum, it's working. I have to say, Harmony, we've never really gotten to know each other before, but I feel like I've known you for a long time."

It was Harmony's turn to chuckle. "I'm so happy to hear you say that, Groundhog."

"It's funny," Mr. Groundhog chuckled, his belly heaving. "You remind me of my younger brother."

"What makes you say that, Mr. Groundhog?" Harmony asked, letting the wand in her pocket slip out of her hand.

"He would always need me to do things for him. Just little things like having me reach for something on a tall shelf or carry something for him. Just to torture him, I would make him do something in exchange, even if he really needed me or even if it was just something I ought to have been doing anyway. Whether or not it was the right thing to do is immaterial. I wanted him to be ready for being older, so even if I would just make him go talk to someone as a part of his errand, I made sure he didn't rely on me to do everything for him."

"How does that remind you of me?" she said, smiling.

"Just the way he knew the right thing to say at the right time. Or the way he asked for my help. I could have just said no. But I didn't want to. Even if I had to do my job as a big brother, I still wanted to help him. That's my brother."

"Where is this brother? How come I've never met him, Groundhog?" Harmony asked. She had already started to think of Mr. Groundhog as a friend, but now he felt more like family. She wondered which of them had started to feel that way first. Maybe it was this spark of kinship that had finally convinced Mr. Groundhog to help her.

"Oh, ho-ho!" Mr. Groundhog launched into another belly laugh. "He's got his own business up north making toys. But I'm not supposed to talk about it; it's a secret thing."

"A secret groundhog toy workshop? I've got to hear more about this one day." Harmony smiled as they turned down the hallway back to Mr. Groundhog's office. They walked casually. Harmony had unconsciously taken the same slow pace as Mr. Groundhog, who waddled while he walked, his bulk shifting from side to side.

"You probably already have and just didn't know it." Mr. Groundhog winked and walked back into his office, leaving Harmony in the hallway. Harmony reached into her purse and took hold of the magic wand. She looked at the elves bustling around the office. And suddenly, she was back in the clearing.

She looked up, confused; the statue was still there. Dawn had broken, and she could see pillars of orange and yellow light peeking out from behind the trees surrounding her. She laid her coat on the wet, spongy grass and sat on it as the sun began to rise. There was a small patch of dirt in front of her. She traced a long line in the soil and drew several hash marks that intersected with the line in several spots. She wrote dates on top of each hash mark: the dates that specific incidents had happened over the last year. She studied the bare earth as though it were a riddle, drawing more parallel lines and connecting them between the hash marks like a miniature athletic field.

Harmony looked up to see that the sun was already behind her, peeking over her shoulder to see what she had drawn on the ground. With her free hand, Harmony rubbed out the lines that she had drawn. She stood up, her back popping as she arched it from side to side. She turned in a circle to make sure no one was watching and, when a small wood sprite disappeared into a doorway leading into the tree, she waved her wand and was gone.

Summary

Increasingly, cybersecurity professionals are being asked to work with business leaders to help address the growing problem of hacking. Cybersecurity professionals usually come from one of two places: information technology or law enforcement. The challenge they face is that, to be successful, they need to be a part of the organization's leadership team, a position which isn't always easy to attain. Furthermore, they're often criticized because they don't speak the language of the business. Speaking business language doesn't necessarily require you to know what "EBITDA" means, but it can help in certain situations. Business language is spoken by cowboys in oil fields, car salesmen wearing plaid sport coats, billionaires in private clubs, and hot dog vendors on a busy street. The common denominator is making money.

Imagine you are the new Chief Information Security Officer (CISO) at a company, and your first item of business is to complete a security assessment of the organization. You've noticed that there are some significant security issues in a particular department. How do you approach the department's employees? Do you require them to change their business processes without first understanding why they run their department the way they do? Do you present your findings to them and leave them to fix the issues on their own? The secret to speaking the business-security language is to partner with department heads and other executives to understand the business's practices and why they're done that way. Then come up with a flexible solution that fits the company's unique needs. Perhaps you need to be able to understand the business better than its own executives do. Perhaps they don't know why they do what they do—they just know that it works.

Takeaways

- Being successful in security means making it a team effort. This requires that employees from across the company be recruited to help you and that they actually *want* to help.
- Harmony had an unlimited number of tries to get the conversation with Mr. Groundhog just right. In real life, this doesn't happen. Things won't go perfectly. Security and

technology people have a different perspective than businesspeople do. So, it's best to approach each other knowing that someone will need to take the initiative and speak the other's language.

Questions

1. How does Harmony's perspective evolve as she begins to work with Mr. Groundhog?

2. Should Mr. Groundhog have responded differently when Harmony first came into his office? Why or why not?

3. Have you examined your business processes to ensure that security is built into them? How can you build security into any changes you make in your continuous improvement practices?

FÈÅ® ØF Å PŪ®®ÍÑG ©ÅꞒ

In a village not too far way away, on the outskirts of a nearby forest, there was a small cottage. Inside it lived an old porcupine. The ends of his quills were all gray with age, making the porcupine look old and wise. He had survived a long time in the forest before finally retiring to his cottage. Occasionally, he would go back into the forest to gather elderberries, just to show all the other porcupines that he still wasn't afraid of the forest.

One day, the porcupine decided to go on a long, leisurely walk. When he opened his door, however, he found a small grass basket on his doorstep. Inside was a sleeping kitten. Its fur was gray and black, and the porcupine could tell the kitten was smiling even though it was sleeping. It purred and purred and purred. The sound travelled up the old porcupine's spine, and he started smiling too. He didn't know why exactly, but he opened the door and brought the kitten inside.

He laid the basket gently on the floor and walked to the cabinet. He picked out a small saucer and poured some fresh milk. The kitten murmured, presumably dreaming of a ball of yarn, but remained asleep in the basket.

Shrugging, the porcupine went outside, locking the door quietly behind him. He began walking and, before he knew it, the sun had gone down. He came home to find that the house was dark and silent. Exhausted from his walk, he trudged up the stairs and tucked

34

himself into bed. He woke up in the morning and went downstairs, but the kitten was nowhere to be seen.

Thinking that he might have dreamt the kitten, the porcupine went into the kitchen to make himself a bagel with strawberry cream cheese. He carefully toasted the bagel, making sure that the toaster was at exactly the right temperature so that the outside would turn the perfect golden brown that he liked. He set the bagel on his plate after it popped out of the toaster, his quills rising a little when he realized just how hot the bagel was. He opened the refrigerator and grabbed the container of cream cheese, which felt good against his burned fingertips. He sat down in the wooden chair and opened the cream cheese but then realized that he had forgotten to grab a knife.

He set the cream cheese back down, walked to the silverware drawer, and opened it. But the silver knife he used for spreading cream cheese wasn't there anymore. In fact, none of his silver utensils were there.

The porcupine's quills puffed out several inches. He marched out his front door and, instead of turning left toward the forest, he turned right and headed into the city. As he reached the edge of town, he passed a piece of paper taped to a light post. On the paper was a picture of the kitten and the words "Wanted: Silver Thief." The porcupine ripped the paper off the pole and threw it as far as he could. Seeing this, several creatures gathered in front of him.

"It was the Silver Fox!" they said.

"Who's this Silver Fox?" the porcupine asked a gray squirrel who stood at the center of the group.

"He always planned to get all of our silver, but he knew he needed to do it all at once. He's the one behind all the kittens. He trained a team of kittens to burrow their way into our hearts and let our guard down."

"Everybody does love kittens," a young squirrel with a moustache confessed. Several of the animals around him nodded in agreement.

The porcupine lowered his head and continued walking, careful to not make eye contact with the other animals, lest they discover that he, too, had a special place in his heart for kittens. He was a proud animal.

He had planned to walk through the town before circling back, unnoticed, to his cottage. He had wooden utensils left from when he had burrowed into his first tree root, but they were nothing compared to his silver.

He realized that he was still hungry as he had not eaten his bagel. And by now, the bagel would be cold and slightly stale. He could heat it up for dinner and make it into a sandwich but, for now, he decided to stop at a small outdoor diner and let the clean air help him forget about the thieving Silver Fox.

He sat down and closed his eyes, drawing in a deep breath and exhaling slowly. He opened his eyes and saw that a small elf wearing a bright red business dress had sat down across the table from him. For a moment, he thought that he may have inadvertently sat at the elf's table, but the elf's smile made him suspect otherwise.

"Hello, Porcupine," the elf said cheerily as if she had been expecting him all along. "I'm terribly sorry about all your silver."

"I, uh, don't know what you're talking about," the porcupine managed to protest weakly.

"The Silver Fox business? He got your favorite knife. Or did I come back too soon?"

"Too soon? What are you talking about? Are you working with him?"

"Oh good," the elf sighed. "I'm not too early. I should have introduced myself. I'm Harmony Evergreen. I work for the Honest Wand Company. I'd like to offer you a job."

"A job? I'm much too old for jokes, Harmony. I just need a bite to eat in peace before I return home."

"Let me explain." Harmony smoothed the cloth napkin in front of her. "Our company is expanding faster than we can keep up with. Eventually, creatures like the Silver Fox are going to come along, just like they did with you, and try and take everything. Can you imagine a future without magic wands?"

"Is that how you knew he got my silver?" the porcupine asked.

"In a manner of speaking, yes," Harmony said.

"But you have all of the magic wands. Why would you need an old porcupine's help? It sounds like you're working for the Silver Fox, and you want to take something else from me."

"If you have to prepare for a future without magic wands," Harmony responded, "then you need to solve problems without magic. That's where you come in."

"All right," the porcupine said, puffing out his quills as much as he could while sitting in a chair. "But why me, specifically?"

"You already know why. The fox didn't know it, but he was teaching you an important lesson. Most people won't listen until after they've lost all their silver. Or gold. Or magic. I want you to teach my employees the same lesson you learned."

"That doesn't make sense. You want to hire someone who was dumb enough to fall for a cheap trick?"

"Yes." Harmony stared at him, all at once very serious.

"And how exactly am I supposed to teach your elves something that you admit can't be learned until it's too late?"

A smile grew over Harmony's face again. "I want you to send them kittens," she said and winked.

Summary

Research suggests that emotion is tied to memories and that our strongest memories are of stressful or negative situations. The CISO is asked to constantly initiate negative conversations within a business. The challenge is to engage in these conversations in a positive way and help solve the issue, not add to it. In a way, this is similar to the role of the general counsel: you probably only ever see your company's attorneys if there is a problem that they need to fix. What people want is to feel supported, and this is accomplished by not assigning blame and by communicating regularly to keep people informed.

Assigning blame creates fear. The best employees in security are the ones who have been through security breaches at other companies. They are the ones who have learned lessons from hackers firsthand. The tendency is to assign blame and get rid of the employees "responsible" for letting a breach happen. But in security, one of the core tenets is that security is everyone's job. So, when security is breached, should everyone be fired? No, of course not. Furthermore, getting rid of a few people who are "responsible" for a problem sends the message that security *isn't* everyone's job after all.

Imagination and fear are very closely tied together. The less information employees are given, the more likely it is that they will begin to assume the worst. Communication is a powerful tool to help prevent employee's imaginations from running wild, but it also helps to build a trusting relationship. The next time that something suspicious happens, employees who trust their CISO will reach out faster to help solve the issue.

You may never meet everyone in your company, and chances are that, even if you do meet them all, there will be some whom you meet only once. Let that impression prove to be a lasting one that can be looked back on as the first step in creating a different mindset about cybersecurity.

Takeaways

- People like watching cat videos. A lot.

- There is one flaw in every computer system that can never be patched or upgraded or firewalled. The easiest way into your company is through people.
- Every cybersecurity incident is an opportunity to teach people that there is a better way. Make sure that they understand the lessons and don't close their ears because they are afraid of consequences.

Questions

1. In a business, how do you balance a healthy skepticism with the desire to break down barriers?
2. After bringing the kitten inside, was there anything the porcupine could have done to keep his home secure?

THE DANCING SALESMAN

Harmony was sitting under the Honest Wand Company tree and studying the lessons she had penciled into her notebook.

- **Great leaders take responsibility for their security from the top down.**
- **Lead by example. This means not asking for exceptions to be made when it comes to security, no matter how important a person is.**
- **Don't tell people to change. Instead, partner with them to solve problems. While you may know all about security challenges, others know how to run the business.**
- **People get anxious about security. Don't use fear to motivate change.**
- **Start at the beginning. Security shouldn't be an afterthought.**
- **Hire those who have experienced hacking firsthand, either in their personal or professional lives.**

Suddenly, the clouds broke and a rainbow began to descend toward Harmony. Its colors were vivid, unlike any rainbow she had seen before. In fact, it seemed solid and tangible as if she could stand on it. The rainbow traveled downward until it ended right at her feet.

A door opened up between the yellow and indigo stripes, and a smallish man with a bushy red beard and a green top hat stepped through. He wore a huge smile and looked at Harmony as if he were an old friend.

The door, which was made of two giant stripes of green and blue, closed behind him and began to fade slightly. The leprechaun waddled the short distance to Harmony and introduced himself. "I'm Chatty McPatty," he snorted. "I've been trying to get in touch with you for some time."

"You found me," Harmony said. "Do I know you?"

"I just want to take a second of your time and introduce myself. You seem like an elf that is coming up in the world. And I hear that you're leading your company into a more secure future. Congratulations."

"Thank you. It's good to know that our reputation for security is starting to get out there. How did you say you heard about it?"

"Just a whisper in the air. The will o' the wisp. If you don't mind me askin', what type of firewalls would you be usin'?"

"Listen, those aren't things that I feel comfortable sharing with someone I don't know," Harmony said.

"Yes, of course. I see that you are as security conscious as everyone has said. Let's start over," the leprechaun said.

"I don't mean to tell you your business, Mr. McPatty, but if you're selling security products, you can't just go around asking people what kind of security systems they have. You should know that's exactly what a criminal would be asking."

"Of course, of course, young lady. You are wise beyond your years. I can see you are far older than you look on the outside. Like you've lived a whole extra lifetime. But even if you could live another lifetime, I don't think you'd find better security solutions than mine in the enchanted forest."

Harmony tried to remember her old life for a moment. She wondered how long had she been travelling. "There are only so many protections that we can build into our tree," she admitted. "It's still just a tree and wasn't really designed to be an impregnable fortress."

"Of course! That's exactly what I was going to say," Chatty said. "Great minds think alike!" He broke out into a celebratory dance, making small movements that could have been mistaken for a seizure had they not been accompanied by a hummed tune. The curly tips of his felt shoes bounced as he turned in a tight circle around Harmony.

"The humans use firewalls, don't they?" Harmony asked.

"Do you know what a firewall is?" the leprechaun said.

"Sure, it's a wall that's on fire," Harmony replied.

Chatty scratched his head, examining Harmony to see if she was serious. "But do you know how a firewall works?" he finally asked.

"I'm not really that technical," Harmony admitted.

"Let me show you then," Chatty said. With a wave of his hand, a firewall appeared. It was a thick wall made of red bricks, several of which were missing, and the wall itself was surrounded by a smoky blue flame.

"What are the holes for?" Harmony asked.

"You still have to let stuff in through the firewall." The leprechaun squinted at her.

"I wish I knew more about how technology works," Harmony admitted.

"Wish? Of course. That's my specialty!" The leprechaun repeated his dance in a small circle around Harmony. He clapped his hands in front of Harmony's face. Harmony blinked several times, stunned, and took a few steps back. The leprechaun had vanished. The grass below her had vanished as well and was replaced by a hard metallic surface. The sun was gone, too. It had become noticeably darker but, strangely, Harmony's surroundings were evenly lit from an unseen light source. Looking around, Harmony realized she was now indoors. The forest was gone. Strange and unrecognizable hieroglyphics surrounded her, glowing brightly as though energy was pulsing through them.

Harmony waved the wand in the air, but nothing happened. Wherever she was, magic did not seem to work here.

A small man in a white spacesuit stepped through a doorway that had appeared in the wall to Harmony's left. Harmony's mouth hung agape—the wall had been solid just a moment before. The spaceman walked quickly toward the opposite wall. When he saw her, he stopped, took two steps back, and said, "What are you doing here?"

"Where is here?" Harmony asked, staring at her own warped reflection in the astronaut's gold visor.

"This is the IO module," the astronaut said flatly.

"What part of the enchanted forest is that?" Harmony asked, looking down so the astronaut couldn't see that her cheeks were turning red.

"This is the edge of the firewall."

"How do I get back to the forest?" Harmony asked, trying not to let her voice squeak with panic.

"I don't know about any forest. Packets come through here, and we stop some of them and let others through. You're not authorized to go any further."

"What's a packet?" Harmony asked.

"It's a piece of a document or some other bit of data. A computer breaks something into smaller pieces and sends it over a network. Packets are each individually wrapped so that other computers know where to send them as they make their way through the network."

"I think I'm beginning to understand what's going on here," Harmony said, folding her arms. "I'm supposed to learn how firewalls work."

"Then you've come to the right place. Our firewalls are forged in the very heart of a volcano."

"Maybe we should start at the beginning," Harmony said. "I have to admit I'm not really sure what a firewall is."

"Well," the astronaut began, "sometimes people driving down the road like to shoot flaming arrows into trees."

"That's mean."

"Yeah, it's pretty inconsiderate. Sometimes people in houses have their windows open, and the flaming arrows go right inside."

"Nobody wants a burnt couch," Harmony said, her voice now more confident.

"You need a firewall so that, when an arrow comes, it will just bounce away. Or, if the arrow sticks, you need to make sure it burns up before it gets in. That's why bricks make the best firewalls."

"We live in an apple tree," she said.

"Doesn't matter what kind of tree you live in. Arrows are arrows. And flaming arrows are the number-one cause of forest fires."

"I didn't know that," she admitted.

"It's true," he said, nodding. He walked to the wall, which glowed when he approached. A diagram appeared, small dots flowing across the picture from one side to the other.

"So we need a brick firewall?"

"Brick firewalls are the standard," he said. "But you still have to have small holes in the firewall to allow messenger pigeons and the strings for any kites you've got hanging in the clouds to enter."

"How do you do that?"

"Smart bricks."

"That doesn't really tell me anything." Harmony pursed her lips.

"You know what a fingerprint is?" he asked.

"Sure," she confirmed.

"How many fingerprints does a bad guy have?"

"Depends on how many fingers he has, I guess," she said. "Probably more than one."

"Exactly. Rather than trying to have our firewalls memorize all the fingerprints of every bad guy out there, we're teaching them to recognize their faces," the astronaut explained.

"Facial recognition?"

"It's just a metaphor. Don't think about it too much," the astronaut said apologetically.

"Where do you put the firewall? Right in front of the tree?"

"It depends. On the one hand, you can't really see firewalls. On the other hand, there isn't really one place you can put the firewall so that it will stop bad guys. A lot of people are putting their businesses on kites in the cloud, so a firewall won't work there anyway. There isn't a perimeter like the one around a castle. You need to put small firewalls in all the different places where your important stuff is. Then you need to monitor all the stuff that goes through the firewalls so you know when an attack is happening."

"But that's like a needle in a haystack."

The astronaut nodded. Suddenly, a haystack appeared in the middle of the room. "Do you know how we find needles in haystacks inside the firewall?" he asked.

Harmony shrugged. "I'm guessing you have to comb through it, but it probably takes a long time."

"You can't fight machines with people. Machines and people think differently, and a machine wouldn't comb through anything." The astronaut nodded again, and an exact copy of the haystack appeared nearby. He and Harmony walked to the second haystack. The astronaut held out his hand, and a small match appeared. He swiped it against his sleeve, causing a small flame to burst from its tip. He threw the lit match into the haystack, which quickly ignited. It only took a few seconds for the fire to consume the haystack completely, leaving a single needle on the ground among the ashes. The astronaut reached down, picked up the needle, and handed it to Harmony.

"That was fast," Harmony said. She noticed a small, silvery thread attached to the end of the needle. "But what's this?" she asked, holding the thread for the astronaut to see.

"We'd better follow it," the astronaut announced. Taking the thread from Harmony, he followed it to a nearby wall, where the thread disappeared into the center of one of the glowing hieroglyphs. "I'm thinking you need to go through here."

Harmony tugged at the string, and the wall rippled as though it were made of water and she could see through the inky surface. There was something else on the other side: another room, but one completely different from the inside of the firewall. It was organic. Pressing her fingertips into the wall, she could feel warm air on the other side. She stepped through. She felt sure that she was no longer inside the firewall. She turned to watch the astronaut, but he had already walked away and was stepping through another wall on the far side of the IO module. She looked at the needle in her hand and, for a moment, was reminded of the wand she had pulled from her father's statue and how small it had been between his fingers.

She coiled up the remaining thread that hung from the needle in her free hand and continued following it through the place she had entered, which was even stranger than the room she had left. This wasn't a room at all but, rather, a giant space with thousands of threads coming from all directions and intersecting with one another. The string she was holding hummed with a regular pulse. Some of the threads looked like immense green vines. Others looked more like transparent tubes that had colorful liquid running through them. Harmony threw the coil of thread she had collected over her shoulder and walked further inside.

She couldn't explain how the word had come to her, but this place reminded her of a jungle. The vines varied in thickness from the size of the stem of a flower to the circumference of a giant oak; some jutted out from the floor, while others were strung at great heights above her, knotted together with hoses. While some threads, like the one Harmony held, glistened with light, others were thick ropes that could have secured a tree in a storm. The floor of the place was soft, but it wasn't like the ground of the forest. Where she expected to step on grass or leaves, there was just a thick green sponge. Light was coming from all around her instead of trickling down from the canopy above. The thread she was holding led her into what appeared to be the heart of the "room," a giant knot made of the three types of fibers: threads, tubes, and vines.

Harmony crawled through knotted intersections of the thread and tubes, pushing them aside like vines in the jungle. There was a bright light coming from behind a tangle of green stems and, when she ducked under a low branch, she could see that the source was a bright rainbow-colored door. The leprechaun stood in front of it, grinning. "Do you like my sculpture?" he asked, clicking his heels together and gesturing all around him.

"I think I get firewalls now," Harmony said, nodding, "but what is this? It seems like it's alive."

"It is. This is what the security of your tree really looks like when you strip away everything else. Imagine the silver ropes are technology. The green plant stems are your processes. And the transparent pipes are your people. They all have to work together to make security work."

"I thought you were just going to tell me how a firewall works," Harmony said. She dropped the coil of thread she had been carrying. The needle buried itself in the green turf.

The leprechaun had produced a pipe and began puffing on it wistfully. "This is the most important thing you need to know about firewalls," he said. "Just because you have firewalls doesn't mean you're secure. If you have technology but forget about people and how they do things, all the firewalls in the enchanted forest won't help you."

"But this mesh that you've created seems random," Harmony said.

"The different parts of the fabric of security need to be grouped together to do things. Security should prevent bad things from happening as much as possible and detect breaches when they occur so that people can respond appropriately. But when things aren't organized properly, security can look random."

Harmony's eyes grew wide as she looked at the woven fabric of the security of the tree, truly seeing it for the first time. "I've still got lots of work to do," she said finally.

Summary

People, processes, and technology are the three parts of every security program. Sometimes, people make the mistake of believing that technology is the biggest or most important part. It isn't. It might be the easiest part since you can make quick changes to technology and buy new things to instantly improve it. But the biggest changes come from people. Changing processes is difficult because it involves convincing people to make changes, but if those people have the information they need, changing processes becomes much more achievable. These three components—people, processes, and technology—need to do three different things: prevent, detect, and respond. They have to do those three things in concert, not haphazardly.

When you think about people and processes, you can't focus solely on the people inside your company. Sometimes you need to look at how your partners or vendors are working with you, which is why you'll need to incorporate vendor management into your security practices. This will require an integration of the legal, purchasing, information technology, and accounting departments. You need to have good security protections in your contracts, but you also need to vet the security of your vendors and have them provide the results of annual audits. Make sure that your vendors don't fall through the cracks, and have mechanisms in place to root out vendors who haven't been vetted for security.

Often, vendors, like the leprechaun, will make cold calls and ask for information they don't need. This is a red flag and prevents you from building a relationship of trust with a vendor. Sometimes this is a pressure tactic to keep you engaged, or it may just be genuine curiosity. But it can be difficult to distinguish between vendors and the hackers trying to impersonate them. Remember that it isn't rude to refuse to give out information.

Takeaways

- Beware of people claiming to be salespeople who ask specific questions about your company and its processes. Trustworthy companies don't ask those kinds of questions.
- Trustworthy salespeople won't disclose their customers' names without prior permission.
- The cloud is neither completely secure nor completely insecure. It has its own features and benefits, but it isn't a silver bullet for your security issues. Like you would with any other solution, be sure it fits you and your needs.

Questions

1. Have you ever received a cold call from someone you didn't know? Did they ask for specific information about your

company, such as what software you use? Did you tell them? Why or why not?

2. What does "deterrence" mean for cybersecurity? Can hacking be deterred?

3. Have you ever heard a CEO state that his or her company is "unhackable"? Is that a deterrent to hackers?

ŦĦÈ ꟓÍŞĦÈ®MÅÑ ØF ฿Í®ĐŞ

Harmony lay on her stomach at the top of a hill, feet in the air. Pressed deep into the tall grass, her body was completely hidden from the prairie that spread in all directions around her. In her hands, she clutched a large pair of binoculars that peeked ever so slightly over the top of the grass. Behind her was the enchanted forest, home to the Honest Wand Company. Other forests lined the prairie around her. To the left was the forest that housed a successful bakery, where elves made cookies and sweet crackers and shipped them worldwide. To the right was the forest where the banking gnomes lived. And at the far edge of the prairie was the forest where the witches were rumored to live.

The grass rustled next to Harmony, but she remained motionless, continuing to stare through the binoculars. Staying prone, the porcupine slowly crawled up until he was alongside her. He then produced his own pair of oversized binoculars and began scanning the horizon. A steady stream of messenger pigeons flew across the sky from forest to forest.

"Have you ever seen one before?" the porcupine asked after some time had passed.

"I've seen everything." Harmony sighed a familiar sigh; it was one that always made the porcupine wonder if he knew anything about Harmony at all.

"What do they look like?" the porcupine asked.

54

"What does what look like?" Harmony asked, now annoyed.

"Giant ogres."

"They look like an ogre. But bigger." Harmony smirked and glanced at the porcupine without moving her binoculars. "Giant ogres have giant nets."

"What for?" he asked.

"I've seen them. They run around catching butterflies in the summer. They also use those nets to catch pigeons."

"How do you know that?" the porcupine asked, intrigued.

"They just did it," Harmony said.

The porcupine saw two ogres following a third, who was carrying a large wooden racket with a loose net trailing behind it. The first ogre snagged a snow-white pigeon out of the air, causing the pigeon to make an awkward leap in an attempt to escape. The second ogre followed closely with a large canvas bag into which the first ogre stuffed the pigeon. The third ogre was also carrying a large canvas bag, but his was covered with small knots that writhed randomly. The third ogre opened his bag and launched a gray pigeon into the air.

"Ogres wouldn't do this on their own. Someone else must be getting these ogres to do it for them," the porcupine said, shaking his head gravely. "Just like the Silver Fox and the kittens."

A line of pigeons glided over Harmony and the porcupine and headed toward the forest. Somehow, Harmony *knew* that these pigeons were headed toward the tree. Her tree.

"We are going to send a black pigeon," Harmony said as she began digging into her large backpack. She drew out a kite, which was folded up like origami. Popping it open like an umbrella, she handed the kite to the porcupine. Harmony then lifted a black pigeon with translucent purple wingtips from the backpack. She put the pigeon into a small fabric cage attached to the kite string. A second, larger fabric cage hung just below the first cage, this one empty and hanging open. The wind caught the kite from the porcupine's outstretched hand, and it was quickly drawn up into the air. Taking the string from the porcupine, Harmony guided the kite into the line of pigeons and caught a pale pigeon in the empty cage. Harmony pulled another string, closing the second cage and opening the first, and released the black pigeon, who took the white pigeon's place in line.

"Black pigeons? That's supposed to be like the Silver Fox?" the porcupine asked.

"Kittens were the method that a criminal used to sneak into your house. Grey pigeons are the same thing, just another way of getting things into your company or getting stuff out."

"If we're looking for grey pigeons then why use black ones?"

"We need to help train people to spot gray pigeons, but it's really hard to tell a gray one from a white one, so we have to start out simple. Black. We can gradually make it dark gray with some black spots, then maybe just dark gray. It needs to be a little tricky to spot and have just enough dark spots to help people find the red flags when messages come through."

Summary

This chapter looks at what happens when messages leave the company and make their way across the Internet. Internal emails are usually encrypted but, once emails leave the company, they fly away unencrypted and could easily be intercepted. Where do the ogres take the pigeons once they've made their copies? Maybe they send them to WikiLeaks. Maybe they go to a competitor or an interested government agency. You should get to know your adversaries just like Harmony did: you don't need to know everything, but understanding their techniques can go a long way. There are a number of email encryption services, but they vary in cost and complexity and usually rely on the sender—or carrier pigeon—to know when they want to encrypt an email and when they don't. This isn't necessarily a bad thing, but it requires users to be educated and ever vigilant.

If your company doesn't already have a simulated phishing program (in which your employees are sent emails that simulate phishing emails and are sent to online security awareness training if they click the links or open documents), then this should be one of the first things you consider adding to your security training portfolio. Such a program can yield huge dividends by increasing the security of your organization; however, user fatigue is a real thing. Sending too many fraudulent emails for training purposes will annoy employees, and they may consider the training a waste of their time. It's also important to take note of how carefully you craft your messages; their fraudulence can be very easy to spot or very difficult. Ultimately, a good phishing email can catch anyone off guard, including me. If a phish is too obvious, lots of people will spot it, and you may give yourself and your employees a false sense of security. For more frequent simulations, focus your training on departments that are often targeted by hackers or users who repeatedly fall victim to your simulated messages.

Takeaways

- Be prepared for data to "leak" out of the company. Being prepared means being able to a) detect a leak when it happens, b) prevent it to the extent that you can, and c) mitigate the damage it causes.
- Emails aren't usually encrypted once they leave your company.
- Get to know your adversaries by following what they do and how they target you.
- Gradually train employees to spot phishing emails: start out with the most obvious cases and slowly increase the complexity of your training over time.
- Focus your training efforts on executives, repeat offenders, and users with access to sensitive information.

Questions

1. Are you familiar with the types of attacks that your company or industry faces most often?
2. Do you know which users in your organization hackers may be targeting?

ŦHȄ Ø®ÍGÅMÍ MÅÑ

The paper man followed a crowd of elves and fairies onto the elevator. As he boarded, small pieces of paper in his knees and waist unfolded like an accordion, making him grow three inches taller. He adjusted the collar of his paper suit, allowing the newly folded pleats to fall nicely into place. He wiggled his shoulders, and a small paper flower popped joyfully out of his lapel. Nobody seemed to notice that he was made entirely of neatly folded pieces of paper. In fact, nobody noticed him at all—not the elves in uniforms or the ones in suits, not the fairies carrying their magic wands, and certainly not the turtle, who moved surprisingly quickly as he walked on his two back feet. The paper man slid to the back of the elevator, making room for several more straggling elves, before the elevator doors shut.

The elf closest to the doors swiped his badge on the card reader and pressed the button for his floor. Another elf standing next to him leaned over, swiped his own card, and pressed another button, which began glowing, thanks to a lightning bug resting peacefully beneath it. "Three please," the group of fairies in the middle of the elevator said in unison. The elf at the front swiped his card again and pressed the third-floor button. The paper man asked for floor fifteen, and the elf once again obliged. The elf continued pushing buttons for each creature present as the elevator shuddered into motion.

The elves began chatting with one another, and the paper man listened intently. One of the elves wearing a suit was either upset or nervous; the paper man couldn't tell which. He was speaking rapidly about a conference-room meeting at the top of the tree. A female elf on the other side of the elevator began asking about the printer problems the company had been having. The elf next to her explained that they had just converted to a new system and had found some bugs. June bugs, lady bugs, that kind of thing. Nothing to worry about.

The elves and fairies filed out of the elevator at their respective floors. The turtle seemed to be in a hurry and barreled out once the doors opened, not noticing that the paper man had stolen his ID, neatly stowing it in one of the folds inside his paper jacket.

After the last elf exited and the elevator doors closed, the paper man's chest began to fold away. Bare paper arms appeared as the sleeves of the jacket retracted upward to his elbows. The elevator jerked upward. His tissue paper lapel began to retract, one fold at a time, until it had become the small collar of a polo shirt. The elevator stopped with a ding at the fifteenth floor. The paper man walked confidentially to the reception desk, which was prominently situated a few feet from the elevator doors. On top of the desk, two dozen miniature yellow buttercups were arranged around a large rose. The display was a work of art.

The paper man approached the secretary and saw the flower arrangement. Near the vase was a card that proudly announced, "Happy Anniversary, Sweetie."

"Well, which anniversary is it?" the paper man asked sweetly.

"It's our twelfth," said the secretary, beaming.

"And he still takes care of you. You are one lucky woman. Anyway, would you mind helping me? I'm still new, and my boss is really upset about the printer problems we've been having," he confided.

"I'm sorry. People are making it out to be a bigger deal than it is," she said, shrugging her shoulders.

"Thanks. What printers do you have on the floor?" the paper man asked.

"Just the one. Take a right and follow the hallway around. You can't miss the sound of the printer. It's running nearly non-stop since Harmony made some improvements a little while back." She stood up and pointed. While her head was turned, the paper man snatched several files from her desk and held them behind his back, where they merged into his paper shirt.

He thanked her with a bow of his head and walked past her desk. There was a small metal cart in the middle of the hallway, and the paper man had to squeeze by. As he maneuvered around the cart, he grabbed several pieces of mail from it. He examined a few of the addresses before tucking them into a slit that had formed at the top of his polo shirt.

At the end of the hallway, as promised, the printer was shunting out small stacks of paper in quick succession. There was a large stack of pages standing next to the printer. The paper man picked these up and held them against his chest, absorbing them into several folds in his shirt that hadn't been there a second before.

He noticed a tall elf walking toward him, and he grinned at her. "Can you help me?" he asked. "I'm running an errand for Sharon at the front desk." She nodded, and he continued, "She sent me to grab some files for her, and since it's her anniversary, I agreed, but I've never been all the way back here before."

The elf smiled brightly when she realized that she could help. "She keeps her files in the file room. It's down this hallway; then it's the first door on your left."

The paper man thanked her as she turned away.

As he made his way down the hallway, he could hear employees gossiping from around the corner. He paused, his face becoming the embodiment of anger, and he shrunk several inches in height while simultaneously gaining several in width. A large paper phone appeared in his hand, and he held it to his cheek. He took several steps back and began muttering angrily in his best imitation of the native troll language. He rounded the corner, and a pair of gossipy elves nervously averted their eyes as he passed.

Letting the file room door close slowly behind him, he changed his appearance once more so that he was again wearing a suit and standing several inches taller. Orienting himself, he ran his paper index finger along the tabs of the files in the room until he found the one he was looking for. He turned and strode confidentially out of the room, the stolen file neatly tucked away inside his well-tailored jacket.

The paper man walked into a large conference room, where a meeting was already in progress. He quietly made his way to a seat in the back of the room. The tables were arranged in a half-circle, and Harmony Evergreen sat near the center, her back to the paper man. Harmony was flanked by Mr. Groundhog on her left and the head fairy on her right. In the center of the wooden ceiling, several mirrors and glass lenses were affixed to small circular twigs. The mirrors and lenses projected what looked to be a treasure map onto a large white screen at the front of the room. A diminutive porcupine stood near the screen, occasionally pointing at it with a small twig. Rather than focusing on the porcupine, who made several excellent points about improving security, Harmony was eyeing an oversized garden gnome seated nearby. The gnome had already cleared his throat several times during the porcupine's presentation.

"Can we get you some water?" Harmony asked the gnome, genuinely concerned. Mr. Groundhog began pouring a glass of water for the gnome.

"I don't need any water," the gnome said flatly. "I don't need any of this nonsense. Don't you see we're wasting valuable time? My team needs to be out there selling wands."

"Wouldn't it be harder for you to sell wands if our customers didn't trust us with their information?" Harmony said.

"Of course it would be," the gnome admitted, "but that's not my department. And after all, it could never happen here."

"Never?" Harmony asked. She nodded, and the porcupine sat down.

Just then, the paper man stood up, walked swiftly to the front of the room, and slapped a file down in front of the gnome.

"Can you tell everyone what I've just put in front of you?" the paper man asked.

"It's my HR file... How did you get this?" the gnome demanded.

"I've only been in the building for about fifteen minutes," the paper man said apologetically. "So what you said about a security breach not happening here just isn't true. I don't want you to take this the wrong way; I'm not saying that your security is bad. Many of the things the porcupine said are actually very good. I just don't want you to have a false sense of security."

"Did you know about this, Harmony?" the gnome demanded.

"Of course. I hired Mr. Origami to help—"

"You need to fire that fairy," the gnome interrupted. "She's the head of HR. I demand an apology." The gnome folded his arms and slouched back into his seat.

"Do you think that the HR file is the only thing Mr. Origami found?" Harmony asked, attempting to conceal a smirk.

"Of course," the gnome grunted. "HR clearly doesn't take security as seriously as the rest of us."

At that, Mr. Origami let out something between a sneeze and a guffaw. When he attempted to contain the sneeze, a staple-bound set of papers containing the sales projections and prospective customer leads exploded from his paper chest. He giggled as though it tickled, which caused a yellow envelope containing paycheck deliveries for the sales staff to flutter out of the back of his jacket. He held his nose, sending all of his paper folds into a wild flutter. Like a bird taking a bath, the creases and folds all puffed outward and, with a poof, hundreds of papers and documents dropped to the floor all at once, scattering across the conference room floor.

The gnome's cheeks began to grow hot and red.

"Is there anything we could have done to stop you?" Mr. Groundhog asked Mr. Origami once he had recovered from the paper explosion.

"You could have made it slightly more difficult," the paper man responded, again somewhat apologetically.

"Why don't you show us how you were able to get in," the porcupine offered.

The paper man nodded, walked to the center of the room, and put his hands between two of the glass lenses projecting their silhouette onto the screen. He deftly moved his hands, and an image of several figures outside the entrance of the tree appeared on the screen. He moved his hands as though reading a pop-up book and narrated exactly how he had gotten into the tree. He manipulated the glass lenses so that different silhouettes were cast onto the white screen at the front of the room. He never mentioned the names of the people he talked to. He was careful not to assign blame to any one group, instead focusing on explaining the technique he used to infiltrate the building and how the employees could have done things differently to make it difficult for outsiders to access private information.

"I have to ask a question," Mr. Groundhog said finally. "I know this is a really important issue, but if we can't stop people like Mr. Origami from getting in, then what's the point?"

"I get this question all the time," Mr. Origami said, bowing low to Mr. Groundhog in acknowledgement. "I've been invited to do this at hundreds of companies, and no one has ever been able to stop me. But I don't have unlimited time on my hands," he said, holding out his wrist and gesturing to his paper watch. "With unlimited resources and enough motivation, anyone could get in. That part is true. But if you make it difficult enough, the bad guys will eventually move on to an easier target. They have to make a living, too. They can't afford to spend months or years trying to get in. Bad guys are looking for a sure thing."

"So it's like a bear in the woods," the gnome chimed in. "I don't have to outrun the bear. I just have to outrun you."

Mr. Origami bowed to the gnome, his folds opening and closing like an accordion. Then, the man folded himself into a large paper swan and, with wings outstretched, he flew out the window.

Summary

Often, after a breach of some kind, companies will undergo major shifts in their processes, practices, technology, and even culture. There are lessons to be learned, both good and bad, that the company's employees will carry with them for the rest of their careers. We call the times when individuals are most susceptible to learning "teachable moments."

The good news is that you don't have to wait for a major security breach to have a teachable moment: you can create your own. One of the best ways to create your own teachable moment is to simulate security breaches. The origami man was using what is referred to as social engineering techniques to simulate how a criminal might steal information from a company by manipulating behavioral responses to interactions. Simulated social engineering inside a company requires a few things, however. First, hacking is a criminal activity unless authorization has been received by someone inside the company who has the authority to do so. You must ensure that your employees face no consequences to for falling victim to the tricks used in the simulation. And although you'll need to communicate with the company's executives and get their approval, you won't necessarily need to communicate the existence of the exercise to the rest of the company. You will, however, need to be sensitive to the operations of the business so that the exercise isn't too disruptive—this is a balance that must be carefully struck. Finally, you should communicate the results companywide, being careful not to assign blame.

When you create a safe way for people to learn, they can make adjustments thoughtfully and incrementally. This will lead to better overall process improvements without the added pressure of responding to a real security breach.

One of the most attractive things about simulated security exercises is that only the ones who are fooled by it receive the training. Identifying repeat victims will help you create opportunities for supplemental training. You should also be sure to incorporate positive reinforcement into the training exercise: recognize those who did spot the phishing message or intruder and provide certificates for those who went through the training.

Takeaways

- Never assume that your security protections are perfect.
- Look for opportunities to create teachable moments about security.
- Never assign blame during a simulated social engineering assessment.
- A company has several areas that can be assessed for security: the building, the computers, the people, and the processes. Assessing just one isn't enough.

Questions

1. What are the top three areas in your company that could benefit from security assessment?
2. Would you expose the employees who leaked documents during a simulated exercise? Why or why not? Would other managers at your company demand to know who they were so they could be held accountable? What does that say about the culture at your organization?

THE INTERVIEWED PIG

The angry-looking garden gnome sat at the end of the slender conference-room table. The polished patterns in the wood ran the length of the table, making the wood grain gleam in the morning light. He wasn't looking at the pig who was talking. Not that he would have made a big deal about a talking pig. He had never seen one before, and secretly he did feel just a little bit special for having actually met one in person. He wouldn't let that affect his decision one way or the other, of course.

The gnome was looking at the sharp quills of the porcupine sitting next to him. Lately, the porcupine had seemed to be Harmony's right-hand man. And after all, it did make sense to appoint a porcupine to security. The gnome didn't like porcupines, though. He didn't really like anyone, for that matter.

There was a long, awkward silence before the gnome realized that the pig had actually stopped talking some time ago. The porcupine had apparently been waiting for the gnome to ask the pig another question. When the gnome blinked, the porcupine nodded and turned back to the pig, who had taken advantage of the pause to write some notes into his portfolio, which he gripped tightly.

"What motivates you?" the porcupine finally asked.

"I really like to help." The pig seemed a little embarrassed to admit this. "I've worked for all kinds of companies and all kinds of creatures. Most pigs are happy to just stay at home and raise a family.

But when I was a piglet, I always went around to the other farm animals to make sure everyone's chores were done. It was just a lot of fun to visit creatures I knew and help them make stuff better. That's what drew me to the newspaper ad about your chief operating officer job."

The pig's voice was magical. It seemed to have little glints of light in it. He had the type of voice that, when most people heard it, they felt brighter—almost soothed. The pig was a little cuter than your average swine but, when he spoke, it was difficult to feel any emotion other than delight. His was the most genuinely positive voice the gnome had ever heard in his long life. But, to the gnome, it was like fingernails on a chalkboard.

"Tell us about a time when you had some conflict with your manager," the gnome grumbled.

"I can't say that I've ever had a problem with my boss." The pig's eyes seemed to flutter when he spoke. The pig was, of course, wearing a pair of red galoshes. His legs were too short to meet the ground from the plastic office chair he was sitting in, so his little rubber-covered hooves dangled joyfully in the air.

"Tell us, then, about a conflict you've had in your life and how you solved the problem," the gnome demanded impatiently.

The pig reached forward and set down the black ballpoint pen that he was holding in his right hoof. The morning sun glinted off his pink skin as he did so. "As you've seen on my résumé, I founded a start-up when I was in college. It was a cool idea. I think it had a chance of making it. Not a big one; it had its problems. Just a shot, but we wanted to take it," the pig said emphatically. He wiggled his hands as he spoke. "So one day, we get this ransom demand. It's from this group that called themselves the BadWolves, a hacker group or collective or whatever. Anyway, they said that if we didn't shut down the company, they would hack us and send all of our business info to our competitors via messenger pigeon."

"What kind of business was it?" the porcupine asked.

"It was a software company," the pig clarified. The gnome grew angry with himself for picturing the pig sitting on a boat and holding a fishing rod. He blinked hard several times to get the image out of his head while the pig continued speaking. "We ignored them at first. Then they sent other demands, and we went to the park rangers. But they couldn't really help. Long story short, they hacked us, and we went out of business."

"I'm so sorry," the porcupine said gently.

"It was partly our fault. We didn't invest enough in our security. It was like a house of straw. Thinking back, anything could have gone wrong and set it off."

"Well, thank you for your time," the garden gnome said dismissively.

"Harmony wants us to look for people who have been through experiences just like this. He was very clear," the porcupine said, gesturing for the pig to remain seated.

"We asked for a time when he had a conflict and resolved it," the gnome said. "Not for when he had conflict and rolled over and took it."

"Oh, I was just getting to that," the pig said, impervious—or perhaps oblivious—to the tension in the room. "After that, I went to work for one of my fraternity brothers. He had gone on to become a doctor and was working at the hospital that his family owned." The gnome rubbed his temples and tried not to picture a little pig in a miniature ambulance. "They brought me in to help upgrade some of their technology. They spent a fortune on security. BadWolves began targeting them too."

"They followed you to your new job?" The gnome's eyebrow twitched.

"They were everywhere at the time," the pig said. "I didn't take it personally if that's what you mean."

The gnome couldn't tell for sure, but he thought he heard a bit of displeasure in the pig's voice, which delighted him. He smiled for the first time since the interview began.

"Actually, they never were able to get into the hospital network," the pig said, which made the gnome frown. The pig turned to the porcupine and said, "We spent far too much on security."

"Huh. To hear some people talk about it, I'd think you can't spend enough on security," the gnome grumbled.

"Have you ever made a house of sticks?" the pig asked the gnome pointedly.

"Of course. And you're going to say a gust of wind could come along—" the gnome began, but the pig gracefully cut him off.

"Even without the wind, houses of sticks have a habit of collapsing in on themselves," the pig explained respectfully. "We changed passwords every day. We installed x-ray machines in all the entrances and put in facial recognition devices. Our website made customers install our own antivirus software to make sure they weren't dropping malware into our network. We thought the customers would love it because we were helping protect them."

"And did they?" the porcupine asked.

"They got excited about the idea, until they found out the hospital was going to start charging extra fees to help pay for it. And then prices went up for all their services. Naturally, patients started going other places. They didn't mind the higher prices for protection, but they would have to stand in line for hours just to get in the place. It was just bad service."

The garden gnome stood up and walked to the window. The sun had almost reached the middle of the sky, and he was getting hungry. An evil thought raced through his mind, and he swallowed hard, trying to push it away. *Bacon.* Smirking, he turned back to the pig. "Are you getting to the point where you did something to change the outcome?"

"Actually, I left there and went to work with my older brother. He had worked his way up to be the president of a very large bank on a farm not too far from here, and he asked me to come in and change some of their processes." The gnome gave in and let himself picture the brother: a smallish but overweight pig sitting on its rump. Over its right eye was a silver monocle. The chain ran down to the pig's collared shirt, the top of which was wrapped in a gray cravat embroidered with large dollar signs.

The pig continued speaking. "I came in, and people thought that I wouldn't spend a lot on security since I had just come from a place that had spent too much. But I helped lead the bank to increase spending on security, not because spending money is the only solution but because the bank understood that trust was a large factor in their business. Their customers needed to trust them with their most precious assets. I helped the executives understand how they were also very risk adverse. I reviewed the company's investment portfolio; they only ever put their money into places that had a low, or at most a medium, risk. Financial bureaus had given the bank their most favorable rating."

"So you stopped the BadWolves without spending too much money?" the gnome asked.

"Not exactly," the pig admitted, still maintaining his cheerfulness. "They did manage to get in a few times over the years. But they were always very small and isolated incidents. And those incidents allowed us to change our processes to stay one step ahead."

The porcupine stood up and pushed his seat backwards to avoid scratching the wood with his quills. He walked toward the pig and offered his outstretched hand. "I think you're exactly the type of creature we're looking for," he said, beaming.

The pig grasped the porcupine's hand with his hoof.

The gnome frowned but offered his hand as well. "Sounds like you're hired. Congratulations."

Summary

You have to understand the risk appetite of your business. This isn't something you can ascertain from the CEO in a questionnaire. You have to know how the company does business, what risks it's willing to take, the type of business it engages in, and how the shareholders feel about risk taking. Many organizations also have a risk department that helps quantify and prevent risks. Some organizations have a Chief Risk Officer in addition to a Chief Information Officer or Chief Information Security Officer.

But when it comes to making decisions, employees in these specialized positions function in the same way as those in any other department: they need to make a business case, and they need to think through cost/benefit analyses of their options. This is an impossible task to do with 100 percent certainty, unfortunately. In addition to the many other types of protection available, companies can also obtain cyber-insurance policies that can help absorb the costs of protecting against digital threats.

As with many other types of security, it is least expensive and most effective to start building cybersecurity from the beginning. This is equally true for the hiring process. Building security questions into the interview process shows candidates that you value security and will continue to do so after they join your team. But you shouldn't stop there. One of the most important things you can do when you bring in new hires is to hold in-person meetings with them in the first few days or weeks after they join your team and discuss the culture of security at your organization. What controls do you have in place (e.g., document classification, oversight, audits, separation of duties, least privilege), and what are your expectations? Having this discussion early on with an employee will set his or her expectations from the beginning and will help the employee contribute to a culture of security within the team and the organization. This is something your employees will carry with them for the duration of their careers.

Takeaways

- You can spend too much money on security. Finding the right balance means understanding what the company values and how it makes decisions.
- Cybercrime impacts every type of business, from startups to big companies and hospitals to banks.

Questions

1. What are some things you can do to better understand the risk tolerance of your company?
2. How might incorporating security-related questions into your hiring processes change the culture of your business?

ŦHÈ ßₑÍÑĐ GÈÑÈ®Åₑ ÍÑ ŦHÈ FØ®ÈSŦ

Harmony was wearing a tall pair of hiking boots and had tucked her pants into them to prevent mud from crawling up her legs. It was a welcome change from the suits and heels she had been wearing every day for who knows how long. A sheath holding a long Elvin knife was buckled into her belt. The porcupine was walking next to her in a similar pair of boots. He held a knotted piece of wood that looked suspiciously like a sawed-off magic wand, the use of which, while not officially banned by the Woodland Creatures Alliance, was strongly discouraged because of its relative unpredictability. The pig followed Harmony and the porcupine. He walked slowly, not out of fear but because he was looking upward in genuine awe. "I've never been in the forest before!" he squealed, not concealing his delight.

"Keep up, Mr. Pig," the porcupine encouraged. "We mustn't get separated this deep into the forest. And you have the fewest defenses of all of us."

"Don't worry," the pig said in his cheery, melodic voice. "Be happy!" He then began humming a song that neither the porcupine nor Harmony had ever heard before. Occasionally, the humming would stop and the pig would repeat, *"Don't worry; be happy!"*

Harmony watched the pig as he shook his fleshy rump while singing. She wondered if the pig's loose-fitting galoshes would give him blisters. Could you even get a blister on a hoof?

"You need to be quiet," the porcupine scolded. "If a wolf or a fox were to see you, you'd be a goner in seconds."

The pig continued dancing happily, albeit much more quietly, as the trio continued walking. The path was marked by tough soil and rutted by hoof prints, tracks, and insects that burrowed in the looser soil at its edges. Bits of grass had begun to creep in as the road became less and less frequented. A tree lay thirty or so feet ahead of them, downed by a lightning strike, the ashes still fresh.

The sound of the wind had been replaced by the pervasive screeching of insects all around them. It was as if the grasshoppers, cicadas, and beetles had chosen that precise moment to form an orchestra. The noise in the woods seemed to slowly grow until, all of a sudden, a single growl caused it to stop all at once. What followed was a silence so thick that Harmony, the pig, and the porcupine began to question whether they had heard the growl at all. Were their minds just playing tricks on them? Then, there was a loud bark followed by even louder growl. Suddenly, they realized that they were surrounded. It was a pack of four wild weasels.

Harmony leapt in an inhuman sprint toward the felled tree. Surprisingly, the pig kept pace with her, his thin, stumpy legs nothing but a pink blur. The porcupine was just barely able to keep up. He ran as quickly as he could, pushing himself along with his walking stick. One of the beasts got a little too close and snapped at him, receiving a chin full of quills. Harmony leapt to a hollow in the blackened tree and put her hand out for the pig, who swung in beside her. The porcupine reached out his stick, which Harmony caught and pulled him to safety.

Just as the growling seemed as if it couldn't get any louder, it was silenced by a trumpeting of horns. Through a hole in the log, Harmony could see dozens of small, blurry figures harassing the pack of weasels that had been pursuing them. Directly below the hollowed-out tree, seven brown squirrels had arranged themselves in a V formation while the others continued to chase the weasels. The three squirrels in the center were wearing harnesses attached to a small wooden sled. Harmony, the pig, and the porcupine looked at each other and shrugged. Just then, a gray squirrel peeked into the hole Harmony had been looking out of only a moment ago, startling all three of them.

"You guys need a lift?" the squirrel asked casually, nodding to the sled below.

The trio dropped to the ground and bolted for the sled. It began moving, and the sounds of battle quickly receded behind them. The gray squirrel easily caught up and took a seat in the sled next to Harmony. "I'm Lieutenant Cedar," the squirrel said, pulling up his aviator goggles to reveal his black eyes. "Sorry about the mess back there. We would have met you earlier, but we had to call in reinforcements."

"No problem," Harmony said nonchalantly.

"Would someone like to explain where we're going?" the porcupine demanded.

"You don't know?" Lieutenant Cedar laughed, smiling at Harmony. "You sly fox. You didn't tell them?" he said, slapping her on the shoulder while flicking the end of his tail, which was hanging over the side of the sled.

Harmony looked disconcerted before admitting, "I must have forgotten to mention it this time."

"Tell us what?" the pig asked.

"See for yourself," the squirrel laughed.

The sled approached a tiny staircase at the base of a giant pine tree. The squirrels unharnessed themselves and scampered off in multiple directions, each one climbing a different tree while Lieutenant Cedar stayed behind. "Just climb the stairs. You're in for a real treat."

Harmony led the way up the stairs, which spiraled around the tree. They had been carefully carved into the thick bark of the tree, allowing the visitors to climb with ease, except for the pig, who nervously grasped the wood as best he could. He was afraid of heights, and it didn't help that there wasn't a railing. They climbed out of the undergrowth and saw a network of ropes hanging between the trees. Each tree held a small tree house, each of them completely different from the rest. At the center was a cluster of structures around a single giant tree, and the staircase seemed to be heading straight for this.

They followed the network of ropes and bridges to the central dwelling and went inside. It smelled of pipe tobacco and wet leaves. Sitting in the center of the room was a large raccoon, his feet propped up on an ottoman. To his right, there was a small draftsman's table with a large, complicated map scrawled on a sheet of yellowing parchment. At his left was a white cup atop a small metal stove. Flickers of light peeked through the holes in the metal.

"Good to finally meet you, General," Harmony said as she extended her hand toward the raccoon. The raccoon returned the gesture without getting up. The pig and the porcupine moved to join them. Although it's always difficult to guess the age of a raccoon, this one was clearly very old. The white whiskers on his chin betrayed him. As the pig and the porcupine got closer, they realized that the raccoon had no eyes, only large, thick scars. "These are my two most trusted advisors," Harmony said, introducing them to the raccoon.

"A porcupine? I never thought I'd meet another porcupine in all my years," the Raccoon said, standing up and patting the porcupine's sides without getting pricked. "But your other friend I don't recognize." He patted the pig's furry shoulders.

"I'm a pig," the pig announced.

"How very nice," the raccoon observed, momentarily distracted by something far off. His black-and-gray ears were twitching, and he made a small scratch on the paper in front of him.

"What's that you're working on?" the pig asked. "It's very pretty," he added with a hint of bashfulness.

The raccoon's attention was once again drawn away by something invisible. Although he was still directly facing the trio, his ears visibly rotated to the left, almost involuntarily. Again, the raccoon scratched something on the paper, this time on the opposite side of the page.

"I'm listening," the raccoon answered, setting his pencil down.

The porcupine silently turned his head from side to side, trying to figure out what the raccoon could be listening for. He noticed that the room was a near-perfect circle. There were eight windows evenly spaced around the wall. For a moment, he peered out the window that the raccoon was facing. There was an old tree covered in moss off in the distance. "Moss only grows on the north side of trees," the porcupine observed, which drew a smile on Harmony's face.

"Indeed it does," the raccoon affirmed. "And what does that tell you?" he asked the porcupine, who was still looking out the window.

"That means you're facing south."

"Correct again, my young friend," the raccoon said.

"Actually, I'm fairly old for a porcupine."

"You're only as old as you think you are," the raccoon said comfortingly. "And you're much younger than I am, at any rate. Pig, do you know what the young porcupine is getting at?"

The pig was a little confused and began drawing circles on the wood floor with one of his rubber boots. He shrugged his narrow shoulders.

"No need to be embarrassed. Did you know that some people call porcupines spiny pigs? You two might be cousins. Why don't you say what you're thinking out loud for the rest of us to hear?"

"It's a treasure map," the pig said simply.

Harmony and the porcupine looked at the pig in stunned silence. Eventually, the porcupine said, "Yes. Yes. The raccoon is listening for sounds from the forest. Each window represents a point on the compass. North, south, east, west, and all of the directions in between correspond to his eight windows. But how did you guess that, Pig?"

"Oh, it was easy. He's got a couple of big red Xs on the picture he was drawing." The pig was smiling from ear to ear.

"Let me tell you all a story," the raccoon began when the awkward silence was too much to bear. "Once upon a time, the squirrels of the forest would scamper around collecting nuts. When there were more nuts than they could eat, their natural instinct was to bury the nuts for later. Have you ever watched a squirrel bury nuts, Pig?"

The pig shook his head no and, somehow sensing this, the raccoon continued. "Squirrels have notoriously bad memories. They forget where the nuts have been buried almost immediately. This is wonderful for the forest since nuts usually grow into trees. But it's bad for the squirrels."

The raccoon leaned forward and grabbed a small twig from a pile under his chair. He swung it around and stuffed it into the metal stove, pausing for a moment to warm his hands. He picked up a steaming cup from the top of the stove and began to sip, the warm fragrance of chocolate filling the room. "I once lost a fight with a cougar and was left for dead rather than being eaten. Somehow I made it to this clearing, and a group of squirrels took me in as one of their own and nursed me back to health, minus my sight. But without my eyes, I was able to listen to their patterns, and I could help them remember where their nuts were kept. There was a huge harvest that year, and the squirrel population jumped. The next generation began calling me their General, and the name stuck."

"So you just listen? And you can find out where all the nuts are?"

"I think I know why Harmony wanted us to come see you," the pig said, winking at the porcupine. Harmony blushed.

"You can't protect your most important things if you don't know where they are. Wouldn't you agree, Porcupine?" the raccoon asked.

"What about the nuts that you can't locate?" the porcupine responded. "Surely there must be some losses that you just have to accept."

"Of course." The raccoon smiled and set down his steaming cup of cocoa. "That's why we have a bounty system. If a squirrel finds a stash of nuts, he gets twenty percent."

"Twenty percent?" It was Harmony's turn to frown.

"Aggressive? Yes. It shows how seriously we take finding all the nuts. The squirrels know that they can't carry all the nuts back themselves. They also know that if they move on from that stash, they'll probably also forget where it was."

"So they need the help of other squirrels to carry all the nuts back to one place," the pig said.

"Maybe it would be better if I just showed you the system we've worked out," the raccoon said as he rose to stand on his hind legs. He led the trio to the opposite side of the room and descended a short staircase on the outside of the tree. At the base of the tree was a tin water pail, its handle standing up straight. As they approached, they could see that a long piece of string had been threaded through the handle before stretching off into the distance. General Raccoon hopped into the bucket and invited the rest of them in. With a shove from several nearby squirrels, the bucket began sliding down into the forest.

The pig poked his head out over the side of the metal bucket. The raccoon stood near the back of the bucket and grabbed the metal handle with both hands. Harmony, on the other hand, sat happily on the edge of the bucket, balancing perfectly in the wind, not seeming to mind the unpredictable swaying. The porcupine couldn't bear to watch and slouched with his back against the side of the bucket, making sure his quills didn't scratch General Raccoon or the pig.

"What about magic beans?" the pig asked as loudly as his gentle voice could manage over the rush of the wind.

"There's no such thing," the porcupine corrected, looking queasy.

"Actually," the raccoon said, smiling, "we find them occasionally. Along with charmed acorns and enchanted pecans. Did you know that when you cut an enchanted pecan in half, it will grow back into two separate pecans? I've felt it happen myself in my own hands."

Harmony, the porcupine, and the pig exchanged a skeptical glance, fearing that some squirrel had been playing a practical joke on the old raccoon.

"Over time, we built a system of nuciducts," the General said. "They are a combination of hollowed-out roots and stone chutes."

"Like the Roman aqueducts? For nuts?" Harmony asked.

"Exactly," the raccoon said, clapping his hands together in excitement. "The ducts have different systems for different kinds of nuts."

"Like for different sized nuts?" the pig asked.

"No, for different *kinds* of nuts," the raccoon corrected. "Common nuts, like acorns, go on top of the nuciducts. They just roll downhill until they get to the collection silos. The silos are usually just hollowed-out trees. They're not safe from bats or birds, but they keep the goats away."

"The special nuts, the ones that taste the best, like pecans and walnuts, we put in a protected system inside the nuciducts themselves. They go to converted beehives that are hanging in the trees around the forest. They're hidden so that we don't have to defend them from the occasional deer or goat, and birds tend to stay away because of the bees. But there's far worse predators out there than those."

The pig shuddered at the thought. He remembered a goat on the farm who was always ramming its head into things it didn't like, which was usually other animals.

"The reason I mention it," the raccoon continued, "is that we put the magic beans and enchanted pecans into their own separate system of nuciducts. These are hidden, mostly running underground in tunnels that the moles dug for us. They run to underground caves where even the most determined beasts can't get them."

The bucket began to slow down, finally arriving at an outpost several feet above the forest floor. The outpost itself was a patchwork of tongue-depressor-sized slats of wood hanging around the edges of a medium-sized tree. Each slat of wood was arranged as though it was radiating outward from the center of the tree.

"What's that?" the pig asked timidly, pointing toward the outpost.

"It's worse," the raccoon said to himself as he leapt from his perch, landing deftly on a branch below. He dove headfirst into a pile of leaves, causing them to fly wildly into the air. Beneath the leaves was one of the beehives the raccoon had mentioned. This one, however, was no ordinary beehive: it had been hollowed out. Inside was a treasure trove of nuts.

But something was wrong. Among the nuts were small cotton-ball-like shapes. And the shapes were moving. From the cloud of leaves, which had yet to settle, spinnerets suddenly shot downward at the raccoon. Spiders. The visitors were being ambushed!

Taking her blade from its scabbard, Harmony grabbed a loose twist of rope from the bucket and tied it around her waist as though she had been expecting the trap. Tucking her Elven knife between her teeth, she ran around the tree to gain momentum and then leapt into the air. The twine caught her fall and pulled her into the perfect arc that would carry her right to the raccoon with the ease of a trapeze artist who had done this hundreds of times. Taking the knife from between her lips, she sliced two spiders in half before plunging the blade into the brain of a third. As she swung back the other way, she noticed that the raccoon had stuffed two spiders into his mouth and was crushing yet another between both hands.

The cloud of leaves had dissipated, and a web began forming above them. In it were hundreds of spiders, and still more were ready to explode out of the nest of eggs beneath them.

Several of the largest spiders began to close in on Harmony, their fangs gaping out of their swollen mouths. At first, Harmony thought the deafening noise she heard was coming from the spiders, but in fact it was coming from behind and above them. The pig had unleashed a blast from the porcupine's sawed-off magic wand. Next to him was the porcupine, whose mouth hung open in a stunned silence. Instead of focusing on one object, the half-length wand had unleashed a broad torrent of light downward, illuminating the undergrowth for hundreds of feet in every direction. The spiders had all frozen in mid-air, their fangs inches away from Harmony's outstretched blade. They hung there for an instant before morphing into tiny houseflies. They attempted to escape but were quickly captured in the webs surrounding the nest.

"Mess with the pig, fry like bacon," the pig said, blowing on the end of the wand.

"That'll do pig. That'll do," the porcupine said, slowly taking the wand out of the pig's trembling hands.

"Some pig," the raccoon said to Harmony.

Summary

To protect something, you must first know both what and where it is. You need a treasure map, if you will, of what your company looks like and where your important data is located. Remember that information doesn't sit still for very long. It can be copied and distributed. Sometimes it's mobile and moves from one place to another very quickly. Whatever form the information comes in, it should be protected appropriately. This requires that you have a classification system with at least three tiers: public, confidential, and secret. Then, you should establish minimum levels of protection for each category. But keep in mind that information can leak out in any place and at any time: an employee's laptop could get stolen, a spreadsheet full of sensitive information could be accidentally emailed to the wrong person, or a portable memory stick used to share files around the office could get left at a coffee shop.

It's common in business to reward great performance with a monetary bonus. To increase the pace of change in security, there should also be financial incentives for addressing major issues. The most difficult part about this is finding measurable ways to reward employees for making security improvements. Tracking security-related metrics that actually measure the effectiveness of your controls is a critical first step. Once you've identified the right metrics, one method could be to create a bounty system for discovering potential security issues. Rewards could correspond to the severity of the issue. Another method might be to begin tracking how effective your security is; for example, you can record how many viruses were downloaded or how many phishing attacks were successful and reward employees who spotted them. Incentivizing changes in behavior like this will have an immediate impact on overall security; however, changes should also be carefully vetted to ensure that bad behavior is discouraged. For example, if fewer issues are reported as a result of employees hiding problems in order to secure their bonuses, your culture of security will be replaced by a culture of secrecy, which will wind up hurting the company in the long run.

Takeaways

- To protect something, you need to know both what it is and where it is.
- Provide incentives (financial or otherwise) to encourage your employees to be vigilant about security.

Questions

1. Have you ever examined how information flows between your department and other departments? Do you know how information comes into your company and how it leaves the company? How could you work to better protect data while it's in your possession?

2. In what ways could you build financial incentives into your organization's culture of security? Would a bounty system work for you? Are there specific metrics you could track

without giving employees a reason to not report security incidents?

THE MAÑ WHØ DÍD ÑÈXT TØ ÑØTHÍÑG

The sloth tiredly hung his head and stared down at the dinner table. He was still wearing a suit from his day at the office, but he had loosened his tie. His wife was wearing a blue dress with a white apron and moving carefully around the kitchen, but the sloth didn't seem to notice. The kitchen was small but clean. Two vintage diner chairs and a small metal table were at one end, and the stove and the sink, both of which were occupied at the moment by his wife's handiwork, were at the other. His wife moved with surprising agility for her species, which brought out a hint of jealousy in the sloth.

"It's not that I'm bored; it's that I'm just capable of so much more," he said finally, continuing his internal conversation out loud.

His wife nodded and set a bowl of vegetable stew in front of him. Several decorative white flowers bobbed on top. She disappeared into the next room and turned on the water to begin the laundry.

The sloth raised his voice so that she could hear him. "I should be thankful; I really should. I do next to nothing. And I don't even have access to the files I would need in order to do more. So why is it driving me up the wall?" He slowly tapped his claws on the table, one after the other, while supporting his head with his other paw.

The next morning, the sloth sauntered into the lobby of the Honest Wand Company, slowly clicking his claws. He was making his way toward the elevator when he noticed his supervisor, an elf, waving at him. She was dressed in a black suit, which was unusual since she normally wore corduroy pants with a fluffy sweater of her own making. She motioned for him to follow her to a first-floor conference room where several park rangers were already seated. The sloth sat down across from them and, to his surprise, his boss quietly closed the door and left.

The park rangers silently gazed at him. They were dressed identically in matching dark-green uniforms with gold stars over their right breast pockets. One was a petite black bear who styled his hair in a kind of buzz cut. The other was a sandy-blond grizzly with a several pink hair berets in her fur. The sloth then noticed the porcupine, whom he had never seen before, sitting at the far end of the table. Next to him was a small rabbit who wore spectacles and was furiously scribbling something on a piece of paper. The sloth correctly guessed that this was the company's lawyer.

"Can you tell us, Mr. Sloth, whether you were working at 2 a.m. last Thursday?" the black bear asked.

"Oh, heavens, no. I was asleep. I'm useless unless I get my ten hours of sleep every day," the sloth said.

"What about at 9 p.m. on Friday?" the grizzly asked. "Would you have been asleep by then, too?"

"No. My wife and I were at a party last Friday. Mr. Pig, the new director of R & D, had a get-together for a bunch of people at the office."

"That's what we thought," the black bear said, cutting him off before he could continue. "We discovered that there was a break-in and some bills were paid to fraudulent companies."

"Oh no!" the sloth gasped.

"And your account was used to authorize the transactions," the black bear added.

On the outside, the sloth stared straight ahead, perfectly motionless but, on the inside, he was reeling. Would he be fired? What would his wife say? Would the company be able to stay in business?

"This is confidential, of course," the porcupine said softly, "but you will probably learn anyway that Ms. Woodchuck was the one who used your account to authorize those payments."

"What? That's not possible. She's too nice to do something like that!" the sloth exclaimed, feeling guilty that he was in the clear while Ms. Woodchuck wasn't.

"Did you ever share your password with her?" the black bear asked.

"I gave it to her a few weeks ago when I had to go to a training workshop. She said the payments were all backed up and we would get in trouble if they didn't get paid on time," the sloth said, tears beginning to form in his eyes.

The rabbit passed him a hanky, adding, "Eighty percent of all crime or fraud is committed by an insider or by a group with a person on the inside."

"And eighty percent of all companies find out from the park rangers that the fraud has happened," the grizzly explained. "Most of the time, the company doesn't even know it."

"You mean she could have gotten away with it? And made it look like I did it?" the sloth gasped.

The warm, reassuring voice of the porcupine comforted him: "You may not have known it, Mr. Sloth, but we limited your job duties on purpose to prevent such fraud from happening. We know you could have done all of the work yourself, but we divided it between you and Ms. Woodchuck to prevent any one person from being able to write checks the company didn't authorize."

"Oh." That was all the sloth could manage to utter. His mind raced, and he thought of how he had complained to his wife just the night before about how he could do more work if only they would let him.

"We also limit what information you have access to. You don't have all the information that you would have needed to commit the fraud," the porcupine explained. "This of course wouldn't rule out any collusion between you and Ms. Woodchuck, but I confirmed that you were at the party with Mr. Pig while we were talking."

As he was leaving, Mr. Sloth walked by and saw Harmony Evergreen sitting outside in the waiting area writing in an old-looking notebook. *The* Harmony Evergreen. Harmony had her back turned to him, and Mr. Sloth was much too embarrassed after what had just happened to introduce himself, but he could read the notes that Harmony had just finished writing on the page. They read:

- Most employees are trustworthy, but eighty percent of theft comes from someone on the inside.
  - Separate critical responsibilities.
  - Give employees the least amount of information needed to perform duties.
- There is such a thing as too much security. To know what the right amount is, you need to understand the business, and the business needs to understand the risks it faces.
- Don't wait to be hacked. Hack yourself and learn those lessons now.
- Security is everyone's job. You can't point the finger just because someone else has a title.
- There should be financial incentives to secure the business just like there are financial incentives for making deadlines or meeting quotas.
- Build a culture that is willing to challenge routines. Make sure such challenges aren't seen as rude.

When Mr. Sloth made it back to his desk that day, the sun was shining through his window, warming his chair. His supervisor came by and didn't say anything—she just patted him on the shoulder and shook his hand. He opened his computer and followed the instructions that the porcupine had given him to change his password. He spent several minutes coming up with a good one that he could remember easily. The porcupine had said to use a long phrase instead of a short, random jumble of letters. Carefully tapping each key of the keyboard with his long claws, he typed, "Separation of duties saved my booty!"

Summary

Separation of duties is an important aspect of security, particularly in areas of the business that deal with accounts payable, payroll, or other financial operations. For smaller businesses, this can be a challenge because there is often only one person responsible for these functions. In those instances, duties can be split among several individuals with other job duties. In addition, regular audits of payments can be done after the fact to ensure there was no abuse. It's important to prevent financial fraud before it happens because, in many circumstances, the money lost isn't recoverable.

Takeaways

- Eighty percent of all crime or fraud is committed by an insider. Often, the company doesn't find out until months or years after the fact. Sometimes, law enforcement discovers it independently and informs the company of the security breach.
- Separation of duties entails purposefully splitting a duty into two smaller tasks and requiring different people to complete different aspects of a job to eliminate conflicts of interest.
- The principle of least privilege means limiting an employee's access to information so that he or she only receives the information necessary to complete a specific task.

Questions

1. What areas of your organization could most benefit from implementing the principles of separation of duties and least privilege?
2. Do you have an existing relationship with law enforcement so that you know who to reach out to when an issue comes up?

ßÅ©k ŦØ ŦHẺ ŞPÍĐẺ®'Ş ÑẺŞŦ

The ACORN system that the squirrels used to store their nuts had, at one point in the past, employed actual beehives. These had since been hollowed out and repurposed, but they still vibrated menacingly when someone got too close. Inside the beehive's paper-thin outer shell was a layer of sticks similar to a squirrel's nest. Inside was a plastic jar with a screw-top lid that the squirrels deposited their nuts into. Despite the intimidating beehive camouflage and the protective casing, the spiders had managed to inject their eggs into the patchwork of sticks as well as inside the seemingly airtight plastic jar. The raccoon picked up a small horn that hung from his waist and began to blow into it, sending a high-pitched tone that, among the creatures present, could only be heard by the pig, who attempted to cover his ears and danced from one leg to another, his face contorted in pain.

Several squirrels arrived and formed a small perimeter around them. "Get the nuts out of there," the raccoon hooted, pointing to the nest.

"Wait," Harmony said. The squirrels froze and snapped their heads toward her. "The nuts could have spider eggs inside of them. That could be how they got inside in the first place."

"What do we do?" The raccoon looked stricken. Despite all the work they had done to protect their treasure, they had failed.

"My team can help," Harmony said.

"We need to know how they got in there," the porcupine added. "We need an inventory of when the nuts were all moved in there and who put them in."

"Why do we need to know who put the nuts in there?"

"Eighty percent of the time, breaches come from an insider. Sometimes it's the nicest elf you could imagine. Or squirrel," the porcupine said, frowning solemnly.

"Actually, the first thing we need to do is to figure out how big the breach is," Harmony explained, correcting the porcupine. The porcupine's cheeks grew pink, but Harmony put her hand on his shoulder. "Just like you categorized the type of nuts and put them in the right type of storage, we need to figure out how many nuts were affected."

The raccoon scratched his head. "If the nuts were infected, there could be other spider nests across all of our storage areas. I should send the squirrels to check on our other stashes and report back. But they won't touch anything," he said, nodding to Harmony.

"Once you know how big the situation is, we'll need to contain it to prevent it from spreading. You'll be in charge, of course, but that means you'll have to decide whether to call the park rangers or not."

"How do we know when we should call them?" the raccoon asked.

"If we think that other creatures could soon face the same problem, the rangers can stop it from happening again. Maybe there's an organized network of spiders that they can help break up."

"What else is there to do?"

"This is where the porcupine's advice comes in," Harmony said, nodding to the porcupine. "He was right that you need the information now, but once you know how it happened, you can prevent things like this from happening again. But it will take all your squirrels working together to make sure there aren't spider eggs inside the nuts from now on."

"How do you guys know so much about what to do after a breach?" the raccoon asked, tilting his head to the side.

"Simple, because we've been hacked." Harmony smiled.

"What? I thought you guys were spending lots of money on security. How can we hope to protect our nuts if you can't protect your magic wands?" the raccoon asked.

"Sometimes, a firefighter's best tool is his shovel," the pig said.

The raccoon turned to him, confused, and suddenly wondered if the pig was a part-time firefighter. He did wear thick rubber boots after all. "I thought firefighters used water," he said.

"They do to put out fires, sure. But for a big forest fire, they'll dig a big, long trench to stop the fire from spreading. If they can restrict the fire to a small area and save the rest of the forest, it's better than trying to put the fire out with water, especially when they don't know how big the fire is going to get."

"So it's like a controlled burn," the raccoon said finally. "In that case, should we just let bad guys into our smaller nut silos?"

"No." The pig shook his head. "But you should focus your energy on preventing the biggest fires. A small fire in an isolated area might put itself out. It'll also have the added benefit of getting people's attention so that they change any bad habits before they could hurt the whole tree or the whole forest."

Summary

Your company will experience a security breach. It's a matter of when, not if.

Now that you know this, you can start preparing for it. Having a plan for what happens during a breach is critical since, when a breach occurs, you're going to be inundated with an overwhelming number of problems: questions from shareholders or the press, lawsuits, and law enforcement wanting to come in and get information from you. In fact, law enforcement may even inform you that you've been getting hacked for months or years without your knowledge. Your plan will need to be flexible to prepare for everything from everyday hacking to the once-in-a-decade kind of events. How will you escalate your response measure? Who will be in charge during each scenario?

When you develop your policy and procedures, you'll also have to make sure that people are aware of them and follow instructions. This means that your policy can't be aspirational. When the lawsuit eventually comes, the standard that you'll be held to is generally the one you set for yourself: did you follow your procedures? Failure to follow procedure can create liability issues. The simplest solution is to incorporate common-sense practices into your policies. Instruct your employees to contact their supervisors if they are faced with a situation they don't know how to handle,

Takeaways

- Before you're faced with a security breach, create policies and procedures to follow when one happens.
- Don't immediately clean up a mess if you don't have to. You've got to examine the mess in order to learn from it. You may also need to preserve the evidence for law enforcement.
- You don't need to stop every attack, just the big ones. But don't let a good crisis go to waste; let it be a lesson that guides your efforts for future improvement.

Questions

1. Does your company have data-breach handling policies and procedures already in place, or would you have to wing it in an emergency?

2. Has your organization experienced a breach (large or small)? What lessons did you learn? Did this help you make needed changes?

THE RUDE TEACHER

The porcupine was sitting in the back of a small workman's van, which had a lightning bolt logo on its side. Inside the truck was a small desk with several black-and-white monitors on it. In front of the monitors was a microphone on a short stand. "Harmony, this is crazy," the porcupine said, pressing the button on the microphone as he spoke.

"This will work," Harmony said as her image appeared on one of the screens. She gave the camera a thumbs-up and then began walking down a long hallway, which was filled with very short woodland creatures of many different species. It was Woodland Elementary School.

"We're not private detectives," the porcupine implored. "We're going to get caught."

"It doesn't matter. If we get caught, I'll just get a do-over," Harmony said, walking around a corner. She was several steps behind a large jackalope, trying her best to keep up with him. He carried a bag of books and swished his bunny tail as he walked, kneeling down occasionally to avoid scratching his antlers on the ceiling. The small woodland creatures' faces lit up as they saw him pass. "Hello, Mr. Jackalope," they called.

"What? What does that mean? A do-over?" the porcupine asked.

Harmony followed the teacher closely. He swiped his card at the door to the teachers' lounge and opened it. The door began to close, but Harmony's hand caught it just in time. She pulled it back toward her and was surprised to see the teacher, his face just inches away from hers.

"Excuse me," Harmony said, taking a small step backward to give herself some space.

He stepped forward, immediately reclaiming the space between them, which made Harmony very uncomfortable. "What do you think you're doing?" he asked, his antlers twitching.

She fumbled with the volume knob on her earpiece and turned it down, lest he hear the porcupine feeding her lines. The little radio she was carrying wasn't really meant to be used like this. She imagined—correctly—that the porcupine would soon be yelling into the microphone and—incorrectly—that his quills would be popping out and shooting through the metal sides of the van.

"I was just going into the lounge," she explained in a slightly apologetic tone as she moved to one side to get around him. He quickly adjusted and continued blocking her.

"You're new here?" he asked, but it was more of a statement than a question.

"Um, yes?" Harmony didn't know where he was going with this.

"Then maybe you don't know the rules," he said. Harmony stared blankly at him and, when she didn't answer, he continued. "They put these card readers up for a reason. They want people who are supposed to be in here to be in here. And everybody else, they want out. Would they have put that card reader in if they wanted to have everyone off the street coming in? Strangers teaching these kids?"

"They wouldn't last a second here, I think." Harmony smiled. "But I don't think anyone would mind if I came in without swiping my card. If we did it like that, it would just take longer to come through."

"You want a snake to crawl in here and swallow a chipmunk?" he asked, clearly annoyed.

"I'm not a snake," Harmony said, wondering how long she could hold out under the pressure of his scrutiny.

"How do I know that? You could be a snake wearing an expensive Halloween costume for all I know." He folded his arms like he had just won the argument. Harmony could tell he would not accept any further discussion without raising an alarm. So she let the door close, swiped her own card, waited for the green light to appear, and then opened the door back up. She walked through, and this time the jackalope let her pass.

Harmony entered the lounge and saw the principal, a small beaver wearing a button-up shirt and striped tie, seated at a small table, a cup of coffee in one hand and a newspaper in the other. When he looked up, his eyes bulged, and he just managed to keep himself from spitting his coffee all over his newspaper. "Ms. Evergreen!" he exclaimed, standing up quickly to shake Harmony's hand.

"It's good to see you," Harmony said, not remembering which of the previous timelines she had sorted through were ones that had led her to meet the Beaver before.

"I'm so sorry. If I had known it was you, I would have asked Mr. Jackalope to stop tormenting you." He stopped and turned to the teacher. "Don't you know who this is?" he asked, incredulity creeping into his voice. The jackalope shrugged. "This is Harmony Evergreen. She's the daughter of the wealthiest businessman in the forest. I didn't know you were coming, ma'am."

"Oh, please, Mr. Jackalope was just doing his job." Harmony waved away the beaver's concerns. "I actually came to spy on him, but perhaps it would be easier if I just sat in during a few of his lessons." For a moment, Harmony looked a bit sheepish.

Mr. Jackalope blushed, his pale cheeks turning the faintest shade of pink. "Of course," the beaver said. "But how do you know Mr. Jackalope?"

"Only by reputation," Harmony explained. "We've had lots of your proud graduates come work for us. Your students, and particularly Mr. Jackalope's students, were the least likely out of all my employees to become the victims of villains who'd try to steal things from our tree. I wanted to meet Mr. Jackalope in person to know more about what makes him different."

Harmony followed Mr. Jackalope to his classroom and spent the day with him. The porcupine joined them, though he was initially reluctant to leave the van as he'd assumed that Harmony's invitation to go inside meant that their mission had been compromised. They spent the day watching the teacher. Once the last student left the room to head home, Mr. Jackalope closed the door and turned to the two of them.

"I think I understand now," Harmony said. "You're teaching people to be rude!" She was grinning. She remembered how he had told the students to voice how they were thinking or feeling when interacting with someone. His students would frequently snap at one other. For example, a young toad prince was told to back off when he got too close to a young princess in training, and a garden gnome made his feelings known when several young elves snuck up on him. Mr. Jackalope would call on his students by name when they talked during his lessons.

"Oh, I'm not being rude. I'm being direct," he explained.

"Like you were being direct with me when you blocked my way earlier?" Harmony asked.

"Just being direct. Nothing personal."

"Exactly," she said. After all, once the children in the class had snapped at one another, they would go back to playing nicely. "You are a really wonderful teacher," she added. He blushed again.

"I think it's called setting boundaries," the porcupine observed. "I've got boundaries too, you know. I'm going home." With that, the porcupine waddled away, leaving the two of them alone.

Summary

People shouldn't need to be confrontational to have better security, but they should get accustomed to being a little more direct. To teach someone to be "rude," you need to follow the same method that was used to teach them to be polite: reward the good behavior and discourage the bad. One of the biggest lessons leaders can learn is to never inflict negative consequences on an employee for reporting a potential security threat or even for challenging seemingly routine requests for identification. You should recognize when someone does something right and set an example by rewarding that behavior immediately and openly.

Takeaways

- Challenging people to follow the rules isn't being rude.
- People adapt to the culture of the environment they are in, so leaders must prevent their employees from discouraging others from adhering to the rules.

Questions

1. How can you incorporate being "rude" into your company's culture in order to improve security?
2. Which of your practices or processes could allow for too much politeness? How could that politeness allow criminals to access your important documents or accounts?

THE TREE OWL

The owl pressed her stethoscope to the tree, her feathered fingers carefully patting the places where bark had been scraped away to reveal the soft, moist cambium underneath. Her eyes flashed bright yellow as she listened. A patchwork of feathers around her eyes suggested that she was tired. Or sad. She moved the diaphragm of the stethoscope up and a little to the side. She knocked on the wood and listened some more. Finally, she pulled the metal diaphragm away and blinked slowly several times.

"Well, Dr. Strigid?" Harmony asked after a long silence.

Dr. Strigid took the stethoscope from her ears and let it settle around her neck. It pinched a row of feathers, making her head look slightly bigger. Beneath her lab coat, her talons were painted bright pink. She shuffled her feet from side to side. "It's a virus," she hooted gently. "The tree has a ten percent chance of surviving. It has an immune system that would normally take care of this, but it may not be able to produce the correct anti-viral enzymes in time."

"Is there anything we can do?" Harmony asked.

"We do make a synthetic anti-viral, but it's only for viruses we've seen before. This one's new, so we have to rely on the tree itself to find the cure."

"But the chances are good that it won't be able to heal itself?"

"I'm sorry. It's a shame because, if the trees could share information with one another about the viruses that are attacking

110

them, they could increase their resistance to viruses to ninety-nine percent."

"But trees can't talk to each other," Harmony said, in part making a statement and in part asking a question, hoping she was wrong.

"No, but you can," the owl said.

"A tree full of elves can't just admit that they got a virus. It's embarrassing." Harmony threw up her arms in frustration. She wondered if the virus would have gotten the tree eventually even if the witch hadn't come along.

"You have to disclose it to your shareholders anyway," the owl reasoned. "You could wait until you fix it, but if you tell the whole forest then everyone else will be protected." The owl tucked the stethoscope into a black bag and began writing on a pad of lined yellow paper. Harmony attempted to decipher the writing upside down, but the owl's handwriting was terrible.

"Like an inoculation against getting hacked?" Harmony said, finally understanding what the owl was suggesting. They entered the tree and made their way down the central spiral staircase. As Harmony walked, elves ran up and down the latticework of shafts and escalators that occupied the center of the tree. Dr. Strigid followed closely behind her.

"Anti-virus is only half the equation," Dr. Strigid cautioned, her talons quickly shuffling to keep up with the elf. "You still need to have a healthy immune system."

"And you think we do in this tree?" Harmony asked. The doctor nodded. Satisfied, Harmony let out a slow yawn. "You probably get this all the time, but was that you in the commercial for the Tootsie Pop?"

The owl hopped into the air and gently hovered next to Harmony, flapping her wings only slightly. "You got me. I did some commercials before plant school."

A huge smile spread over Harmony's face. "I always wondered why I didn't see you in more commercials."

"The market for cartoon owls just dried up one day, and I got laid off." She shrugged. "So I went back to school like my parents always wanted." She fluttered along the spiral staircase while Harmony ascended, boots knocking on the steps.

"That was such a good commercial. I still think about how many licks it takes to get to the center of a Tootsie Pop." Harmony gripped the rail and looked up at the steps ahead.

"Oh, that's an inside joke," she laughed. "I gave you the answer."

"But you just counted to three."

"No. I said, *Wa-hun. To-who. Three. Three.* I was spelling out the whole number: one thousand two hundred and thirty-three. It takes exactly that many licks to get to the chocolate center."

"That's crazy. The answer was there the whole time," Harmony gasped.

"Actually, this whole virus problem reminds me of this movie I worked on. I was in this giant ballroom with hundreds of other characters dancing around. There were several invisible fairies flying around and stealing people's wallets. A person might notice something and scream, but by then the fairy was gone."

"That sounds like a terrible movie."

"It was this artsy French thing. Since it was a party, they all had little bits of confetti. One of the characters, a panda on a unicycle, saw a wallet float out of a lioness's handbag and tossed the confetti at it. The confetti stuck to the fairy, and everyone else could see her." They stopped at a hole in the tree, which leaked daylight onto the floor below. Dr. Strigid stepped into the sun, gently closing her eyes as she warmed herself.

"How does that apply to the tree situation?" Harmony asked.

"Well, it doesn't help the tree," she said, "but it does help the forest. In the animal kingdom, we call it herd immunity. If enough of the animals are immune then the sickness, or whatever it is, is starved out of existence."

Harmony peered out of the hole in the tree and looked out across the forest surrounding them. She knew almost all of the neighboring elves. She knew some of the squirrels who lived in the pecan trees by the stream. She knew a few of the birds who made their homes at the tops of the pines that towered over the other trees in the denser parts of the woods. But she had never told them about what was going on inside her tree. They were the competition. Plus, she had a reputation to maintain.

"Even if the tree survives this virus," the owl continued, sensing her thoughts, "there will be others. There won't be cures for all of them."

"But…" Harmony hesitated. "Why can't we just call the park rangers? Shouldn't they be the ones to figure all this out?"

"There are lots of different parts of the immune system," the owl countered.

"What does that mean?" Harmony asked, folding her arms.

"A healthy immune system has five parts. The park rangers are like the white blood cells. They go and attack an infection, but usually that only happens after the damage has already been done."

"I'm beginning to understand," Harmony said. "What are the other parts of the immune system?"

"First, everybody has antibodies that destroy foreign substances and compliment the work of the white blood cells."

"Like how we have the porcupine in charge of fending off attacks against the tree?" Harmony asked.

"Exactly," she said.

"That's two parts. You said there were five?"

"The lymphatic system. It carries nutrients between the cells themselves and the bloodstream. It has a network of nodes, and the lymph fluid helps trap the foreign substances so that special white blood cells can attack them."

"I'm not sure what part of the tree that would be," Harmony admitted, shuffling her boots on the dusty wooden floor.

"The humans have something called the Internet," the owl answered. "It's how they communicate. Information flows throughout a network of computers. And they sometimes use it to capture information about the bad guys."

"Interesting," Harmony said. "Maybe we can figure out where the bad guys are coming from and which computers they're targeting. What's the next part?"

"Well, where do you think the body gets all those white blood cells and antibodies?" the owl hooted. "Bone marrow produces white blood cells, and the tonsils produce the antibodies."

"I can't think of where those fit into the picture, either," Harmony said, more frustrated than ever.

"What about the tree colleges?" Dr. Strigid suggested.

"That makes sense. We need people who have training in this stuff and know all the basics already!" Now it was Harmony's turn to jot down a note. "So what's the last part?"

The owl lifted her wing and pecked at several feathers that were sticking up, smoothing them back down. When she raised her head, she said, "The spleen filters the blood, removes all the old, damaged cells, and helps destroy bacteria directly."

"I think I'm getting the hang of this. This is like our internal protections inside the tree: like firewalls, spam filters, penetration testing, and centralized logging."

Harmony fished through her purse and pulled out her old spiral notebook. It was heavily worn, and the pages were starting to pull away from the metal spring that held them together. She turned to the last page and began writing, careful to think about not just the lessons she had learned but the lessons that other people had learned and told her about:

- **Don't trust vendors to do security for you.**
- **Make a map of how and where your business uses information. You can't protect information if you don't know where it is.**
- **Sometimes a firefighter's best tool is his shovel.**
- **Small fires can help prevent larger fires.**
- **Communicate openly about issues, both inside and outside the company. Participate in groups that help prevent both competitors and partners from being hacked.**
- **Law enforcement is only one part of the immune system that protects against threats. Develop a healthy business immune system that has many parts.**

When she finished writing, Harmony added the following notes:

Security is like a company's immune system. There are five parts:

- **External security**
- **Internal people and processes**
- **Communication and intelligence sharing**
- **Employee training and degree programs**
- **Internal technology protections**

"But all of this is just theoretical," Dr. Strigid confessed. "You were right that it will take a huge change to get all of the trees to talk to each other."

"I think I can help with that." Harmony reached into her purse and took hold of the wand. She would have to go back even further in time if she was to have enough time to build a network of trees before the virus could take hold. But there it was: a narrow glimmer of hope that she might finally turn the tide of threats, all of which seemed to end with the company going out of business or her father being replaced by a statue.

<u>Summary</u>

Every time I interview a candidate, I ask, "Who is your role model in cybersecurity?" Some candidates name great hackers, and others will choose a journalist or a prolific researcher. Compare these answers to a businessperson's heroes: Jack Walsh or Henry Ford, Warren Buffet or Stephen Covey. This highlights a stark difference between the security industry and other industries: there are very few examples of leaders who are widely known and recognized throughout the security community.

The issue is communication. The work that great security leaders perform isn't just not talked about; it's kept secret. Every day brings new examples of great leaders who have prevented their businesses from being hacked, but those examples are hidden from the business community. We don't want to talk about our defenses because then the bad guys will know how to circumvent them. While this is a very logical position, it creates a vacuum of leadership and a cycle of secrecy that ultimately prevents the security community from becoming a partner to the business community. Many industries have already implemented information-sharing groups, called Information Security Advisory Councils, but these are generally industry-specific and don't bring in intelligence from other industries.

IT people often approach security problems using a completely different language than the one that businesspeople use. When sharing information company-wide, my advice is to use analogies, which makes communication easier and more productive. Analogies don't just ease communication; they help spark ideas that resonate with all employees, regardless of their department.

Takeaways

- Security is like a body's immune system. All of the parts must function together to be effective.
- Communication between companies, even between competitors, is essential to forming herd immunity against cybercriminals.

Questions

1. Is your company a member of your industry's Information Security Advisory Council (ISAC)? Does your industry have an ISAC?
2. Is your company's security immune system working effectively?

THÈ WØMÅÑ WHØ FØŪÑÐ HÈ®$È£F

Harmony drew in a deep breath. She was sitting cross-legged in the clearing outside of the Honest Wand Company tree. The wind was light but steady, gently bending the blades of grass around her. It would have been a nice day to fly a kite. She held the wand in her hand like a pencil, twirling it between her thumb and forefinger, first clockwise and then counterclockwise. It felt lighter. In truth, it was nearly out of magic. Even after spending many years around magic wands, both making them and using them, she had no idea exactly how long one lasted. And yet, holding this one in her hands, she knew there was only one wish left in it.

She couldn't say how much time she had spent making wishes to go back in time. Going back and fixing the damage of several different problems had taken a toll on her. Just how many wishes had she made? She tried to count them all but couldn't. She thought about all the people she had met but, again, she lost track. She had only spent three wishes and a few hours when she met the porcupine to get it right, but she must have spent weeks of wishes with Mr. Groundhog. Could she have spent years making wishes?

Was it enough?

An elf was sitting a little distance away from her, his face beaming upward at the sun. In one of his hands was a knife and in the other was a small stick. The bark of the stick had been whittled away, and the elf was absentmindedly pressing the knife into the wood.

It was a young Honest Evergreen.

As her father continued to whittle, Harmony could see the signature Honest Wand bumps beginning to form in the wand's handle. Harmony lay back in the grass and looked up at the sky. The clouds gliding past made her feel lonely again.

As she returned to watching her father, she realized something. Honest wasn't working; he was enjoying himself. He was doing what he loved. And, after all the time she had spent working to fix her father's company, Harmony realized something else: she was enjoying herself, too. She knew how to fix the company now, and all it would take was a little planning and decision making. Things worked. They didn't work flawlessly—there were problems here and there—but, all in all, Harmony knew everything would be okay. Now, they would learn from their mistakes.

A frog hopped to Harmony's side and began tugging away at the wand.

"There's only a little left in it, my friend. I can't make you into a prince." Harmony smiled at the frog, who was looking expectantly at her. Was he puckering up for a kiss, or was it just her imagination? "I tell you what I'll do. I'll give you a voice that you can use to sing to people. You will tell stories through your songs, and you'll make them remember days like this one." She waved the wand sideways at the frog, who stood up and took a respectful bow. With one arm tucked behind its back, it walked quickly away while humming a familiar tune. *"It's not unusual to be loved by anyone. It's not unusual to have fun with anyone."*

"It's time to go home, my friend," Harmony said to the wand.

The wand began to glow white. Harmony held out her hand as the glow continued to get brighter. She gripped the wand tighter but found that she could no longer feel it in her hand. She turned her head away and closed her eyes, but the whiteness continued to expand so that the light poured through her tightly shut eyelids and invaded her mind.

The world faded away and, for a moment, Harmony thought that she was falling. No, not falling. Flying. The wand was accelerating away from her, and she was holding on as tightly as she could. It was all she could do to keep her fingers bent around it. She began accelerating faster and faster until she heard a loud boom. Harmony's strength gave way, and the wand slipped from her fingertips.

The sensation of movement abruptly stopped. The blinding light had also vanished, and Harmony carefully opened her eyes. She was in the clearing again but, as her eyes adjusted, she realized that it was now dusk. She was facing a giant statue of Honest Evergreen, whose arm stretched out in front of him as if he was holding a magic wand. Harmony was standing near the base of the statue and had to crane her neck upward to look at it. She peered at the tip of her father's hand but couldn't see whether the magic wand was up there.

A warm hand clamped down on her shoulder. "Welcome back," she heard someone behind her say. It was Honest Evergreen. Harmony had almost forgotten the sound of her father's voice.

When Harmony turned around, it wasn't just her father she saw. Surrounding Honest Evergreen were hundreds of elves and other woodland creatures. A fairy hovered near Honest's right shoulder. A porcupine stood a little further away, and Mr. Groundhog was next to him, a patterned red tie hanging around his neck. The tree owl and Mr. Jackalope and the raccoon and the pig were there as well. It seemed as though everyone from the company was standing before her; in fact, there were too many creatures to count. Had the company grown?

Seeing the look in Harmony's eyes, her father said, "We invited our employees and their families, our customers, and our shareholders. They all came today to celebrate what the company has become. All thanks to you, Harmony."

"It wasn't just me," she said quietly. "It was everyone."

Her father smiled. "Spoken like a true Evergreen."

"Really," Harmony said emphatically. "I knew what the tree would have looked like if we didn't at least try to change things. It just took me helping everyone to understand. But that was the easy part. It took everyone working really hard to make all the changes."

"You mean, to prevent the future where I was turned to stone by an evil witch?" Honest winked at Harmony.

"You remember?" Harmony asked.

"Of course." Honest smiled warmly. "I wished that you would protect the company, and you did. I knew that if I tried to stop the witch by myself, it would end up just hurting the company. Not just the company, actually. The people of the company would be the ones most hurt. In that moment, I realized that magic couldn't save the company. It would take everyone working together."

Just then, a giant witch appeared in the clearing. The sun was beginning to set.

"Dad, it's the witch. What do we do?"

"Relax, Harmony. Who do you think made this new statue for us? She's now one of our biggest shareholders."

The witch waved a giant magic wand, and thousands of lightning bugs appeared. A band materialized at the foot of the statue and began playing a surprisingly danceable tune. The lightning bugs began to circle the statue of Honest Evergreen, their glowing light pulsing rhythmically.

When the crowd began dancing, Harmony looked down at her feet. "What's wrong?" Honest asked. "This is your party. We've been waiting for this day for a long time."

"I just don't know. What do I do now?" Harmony asked.

"Maybe you should write down all of the things you learned so that other companies can benefit from what you know."

Harmony looked back at the notes she had compiled in her notebook:

- **Great leaders take responsibility for their security from the top down.**
- **Lead by example. This means not asking for exceptions to be made when it comes to security, no matter how important a person is.**

- Don't tell people to change. Instead, partner with them to solve problems. While you may know all about security challenges, others know how to run the business.
- People get anxious about security. Don't use fear to motivate change.
- Start at the beginning. Security shouldn't be an afterthought.
- Hire those who have experienced hacking firsthand, either in their personal or professional lives.
- Most employees are trustworthy, but eighty percent of theft comes from someone on the inside.
    - Separate critical responsibilities.
    - Give employees the least amount of information needed to perform duties.
- There is such a thing as too much security. To know what the right amount is, you need to understand the business, and the business needs to understand the risks it faces.
- Don't wait to be hacked. Hack yourself and learn those lessons now.
- Security is everyone's job. You can't point the finger just because someone else has a title.

- There should be financial incentives to secure the business just like there are financial incentives for making deadlines or meeting quotas.
- Build a culture that is willing to challenge routines. Make sure such challenges aren't seen as rude.
- Don't trust vendors to do security for you.
- Make a map of how and where your business uses information. You can't protect information if you don't know where it is.
- Sometimes a firefighter's best tool is his shovel.
- Small fires can help prevent larger fires.
- Communicate openly about issues, both inside and outside the company. Participate in groups that help prevent both competitors and partners from being hacked.
- Law enforcement is only one part of the immune system that protects against threats. Develop a healthy business immune system that has many parts.

Harmony paused and thought about all of the people she had met, the team she had brought together to solve the challenges that arose, and the company she loved, and she began writing in her notebook.

A long time ago, in a land not so far away, people thought that the wave of a magic wand could solve all of their problems. But one day there weren't any more magic wands, and everyone was afraid. All the messenger pigeons in the land carried news of trees that had all their fruit picked in the middle of the night while the woodland creatures were sleeping. It was a dark time in the forest, and every elf, gnome, and fairy was afraid of what the future held. But when they worked together and followed a few simple rules, they realized they didn't need magic to solve their problems after all.

Summary

Harmony was almost surprised at the response she got at the reception. She didn't know it, but her father, the founder and president of the company, had been watching, knowing that she had been making changes behind the scenes. Harmony didn't make these changes to be recognized for them but to save the company. Security is something that should be recognized and celebrated. When people feel appreciated, achievements are set apart and made into an event. When achievements are recognized in an honest and sincere way, it is something that people will remember forever. And cybersecurity is something we need everyone inside our companies to think about all of the time. Can your organization host an annual cybersecurity awards dinner where you fly people in from all around the country to celebrate your progress? How do you think that would affect the commitment to improving cybersecurity at your company?

Harmony was a high-level executive in her company and had broad authority to make changes because she was the daughter of the founder. To be successful, there must be an executive sponsor or sponsors willing to commit to a long process of change and who can accept that some of those changes may be major ones for the company. How can you get that commitment? Spread the word. Follow in Harmony's footsteps and write your own story down and share it inside your company, perhaps in a cybersecurity newsletter or blog. Discuss it with your peers at other companies. Share the message.

Takeaways

- Although Harmony may have thought she was working solo in making wishes and going back in time to make changes, she wasn't working alone. She had built a team around her from all over the company.
- Recognition reinforces the message that cybersecurity is important to your company and creates a lasting impression on your employees.
- Transformative cybersecurity change can't stop with you. Pass this book along to others and create a forum to share stories with people inside your company.

Questions

1. If you could change three security-related decisions that you made over the last several years, what would they be?
2. What's stopping you from making those changes now?
3. Who do you know in your organization that you could partner with to help make those changes?
4. Can your company host an annual event—modest or extravagant—to recognize people throughout the company who have had an impact on improving cybersecurity?
5. Who else inside your company could benefit from reading this book or from hearing your story about cybersecurity change? Who would you share this message with outside your company?

GEORGE FINNEY, ESQ., has worked in Cybersecurity for over 15 years. He is currently the Chief Information Security Officer for Southern Methodist University where he has also taught on the subject of Corporate Cybersecurity and Information Assurance. Mr. Finney is an attorney and is a Certified Information Privacy Professional as well as a Certified Information Security Systems Professional and has spoken on Cybersecurity topics across the country.

Made in the USA
Lexington, KY
06 June 2018